DELIVERING
A
NEW
WORLD
ORDER

Book 2   Mark Warburton

Mark Warburton is....

A former Atlantic Regional Manager for QSP Inc., servicing the fund-raising needs within the public school systems of each respective Atlantic Canadian province.

An innovator-owner at MAGpi COMMUNICATIONS Inc. – author of a prototype publishing program for the public school sector.

More to the point of this book, Mark's true passion has grown out of his lifelong association with Jehovah's witnesses. This passion presents as an elevated appreciation for love, justice and the empowerment of all true Christians in pursuit of the only NEW WORLD ORDER that can work, for the benefit of humankind.

The book is a distillation of his collection of letters, penned to appointees within the CCJW, numbering into the hundreds and written over a period 25+ years, documenting both the tragedy of his ostracism from family and friends and the slippage of a noble movement. It weaves historical aspects of the undertaking, organizational miscues and key leadership issues into a commentary that sheds light on both the original timber of the movement and on the reasons for the grave challenges it now faces.

It is a book of lessons learned, of emergent opportunity, of HOPE.

Psalm 43...of the Sons of Korah

1. Declare me innocent, O God,

   And do conduct my legal case against a

   nation not loyal. From the man of deception

   and unrighteousness may you provide me with

   escape,

2. For you are the God of my fortress

   Why have you cast me off?

   Why do I walk about sad because of the

   oppression of the enemy?

3. Send out your light and your truth,

   May these themselves lead me,

   May they bring me to your holy mountain and to

   your grand tabernacle,

4. And I will come to the altar of God,

   To God, my exultant rejoicing,

   And I will laud you with the harp, O God my

   God.

5. Why are you in despair, O my soul,

   And why are you boisterous within me?

   Wait for God, for I shall yet laud him as my

   Grand Salvation and as my God.

Table of Contents

TO MY READERS:

"…. what goes up, must come down….

spinnin' wheel gotta go round…."

David Clayton Thomas - BS&T

As I read the Toronto Star this morning, I see that our bankers are defending against the story which broke a few months ago. Frontline people at their respective banks, of which my sweet wife is one, revealed that the pressure to sell made them feel uncomfortable about their roles in dealing with the public. For the benefit of the politicians who had assembled to take a look at this sordidpractice, of course, the reassurance from the banker people is that "the banks strongly denied that such accusations were part of their cultures…., yet, occasional cases of inappropriate behaviour are possible, since the institutions are massive operations ….".

And, on the latest in the gender wars, the headline reads, "Madrid Bans Manspreading On Bus Transit"   on two occasions now, while riding the bus here in Hamilton, I have had young women take issue if any part of my body infringed on their space…. on public transportation, no less!

This old world is, indeed, a mélange of special interests, each vying for somedisparate, conflicting form of justice. Legal systems exist to referee and to quantify damage, the media tracks an endless catalogue of complaints, politicians ride the waves, and the world keeps spiralling to new depths.

As soon as I could understand, I was introduced to a New World Society. My parents, John and Rita, subscribed to an alternative world - a world where mutual respect between lovers of God meant that there was no dispute that could not be resolved, no interest that could not be accommodated. After all, this New World Society was not just another religion!...in fact, it was not a religion at all!

Such was their commitment to the cause of this brotherhood, that in 1956 our small family was uprooted from our hereditary home in the Wales/Northern England locale, and sent hurtling on the great adventure of a move across the Atlantic to Hamilton, Ontario, Canada. This was all in pursuit of our eventual attendance at Yankee Stadium in 1958, at the grandest gathering of Jehovah's Witnesses ever held.

During the convention, which lasted 8 days, from Sunday to Sunday, we stayed with a family in an apartment building, the likes of which I had never seen, 40 stories, perhaps, deep in the bowels of New York City. These humble people of colour had graciously offered accommodation to visiting delegates for a pittance, I am sure. Sessions at the convention were held each morning, afternoon and evening. What an experience!

The promise of the New World Society was for a revolution in the practise of Christianity….and we bought into it, hook, line and sinker. I cannot think of any other couple who took this hope more seriously than my parents.

This series of books is dedicated to the memory of John

and Rita. Both have passed on in recent years, and like many others, their hope for a New World Order, as promised in the Bible, burned bright. Unfortunately, they passed withoutever seeing their hope fulfilled. Sadly, as hard as they, themselves, tried to live upto the guiding principles of this burgeoning movement, their high hopes of a caring and just brotherhood degraded around them. The Christian Congregation of Jehovah's Witnesses let them down.

This book is necessarily based on my personal experience as a Jehovah's Witness. It is an attempt to explain why the hope instilled in me by my parents has been, so far, frustrated; how the high ideals of a protest movement against religious hypocrisy morphed into a mirror image of the Catholic Church. It is an endeavour to understand, by penning my deepest contemplations on the matter,just how we might get back to what we once were. Nae, I am working to understand how a movement commissioned by God himself, prophesied about by Jesus Christ, and brought to life against all odds by Charles Taze Russell might become the catalyst it was intended to be, for entry into the New World Order, the Kingdom of Jesus Christ.

Thank you for your kind attention.

Mark Warburton

June 12, 2017 - Hamilton Ontario Canada

CHAPTER 1: THE CHALLENGE WE FACE

The secular, or the scientific world is impressive, indeed.

Considering the parochial patterns of a world guided by the religious moralities which have dominated thought, and action, throughout history, the secular systems developed in our "age of reason" are remarkably even-handed. If it were not so ironic, we might designate these systems, and the discipline of scientific thought, to be a "godsend".

I ponder the ongoing coronavirus pandemic, still threatening us as I form these thoughts, and, more to the point, I consider the scale on which enlightened authorities have imposed a coordinated secular solution. As pointed out in an unusually prescient FB post that I read early on in this crisis, the authorities mustered and imposed a global shut-down - of movement, of assembly, of precious individual rights - to contain what has proven to be a killer of less than 2% of its' victims – impressive controls, replete with police apprehension and bizarre financial penalties (fines), and frightening, too.

The scale of the operation is its salient feature; in actuality, it mirrors the scope of all of mankind's challenges. Where are we not threatened? Global warming, global economics, global disease, another global war, global everything.......

Now, if religious systems have historically been self-serving and usurious, what can we say about the allocation of resources within the secular authority? If such authority does, in fact, hold promise of an answer to the multi-dimensional, intricately woven bane of the human condition, what might the cost be? By any slide-rule, by any supercomputer, by any calculation, the secular system is no more sustainable at the rates we have seen than the non-rational and opulent religious authority which it has supplanted.

The Director of the WHO (World Health Organization) is quoted as saying that the "eight pillars" of WHO healthcare will save the day, this time, and, by implication, forever. At the same time, the UN Court of Human Rights promises attention to deficits of justice around the world, and the chastened religious community, having had its moral dominance wrested away, speaks through suchtrollops as the World Council of Churches. It suggests a coming-together in matters spiritual, meaning, sadly, tolerance of every aberrant behaviour, and about religion, generally, we might say that is a tarnished facet of the jewel onceseen to be the global solution to mankind's dysfunction (ya know, the 4+1 "estates"). Religion, in its current impotent state is not much more relevant forglobal solutions to global problems, than the feudal second estate, the Monarchy.

The trajectory of these secular efforts promises only higher costs.....the pomposity, the opulence and the expense of feudal religion is a flea compared to the elephantine costs of a voracious secular system, consisting of many strata of governance, from city hall to the global authority envisaged as part of ANOTHER NEW WORLD ORDER (not the NWO of which we speak herein), intent on accommodating every permutation of human expression - culture, religiosity, gender splintering, etc, etc, ad infinitum.

I am reminded here of a longstanding disharmony with my first son about the principles of human organisation - our dispute is known as the "data warehouse"approach versus the "organised flow chart". Without revealing the exact personal nature of this grave philosophical debate, let us say that the systems of mankind are severely taxing the "warehouse" capacity of human resources, and that a svelte, streamlined "flowchart" must guide us to better use of the finite global resources available to us.

In this, our second contemplation on DELIVERING A NEW WORLD ORDER, we return to the perspective and the hope, the flowchart, laid upon us by none otherthan Jesus Christ.

CHAPTER 2: AN ESTATE FOUNDERING AND LOST

The first of the "Estates" of our western world, the church leaders of Christendom, are in turmoil. While espousing a coming together and mutualrespect, and while including in such a melding an emasculation of Christian standards, the religious leaders of our day now offer the same benign reassurances that one might expect from a politician.

Never mind that the great preoccupations of this world, namely, business, sports, politics, science & art carry on apace, and the attendant Fourth and Fifth Estates (the press & the outlier media) continue to, often breathlessly, document and qualify. The First Estate was supposed to be the moral anchor which promised to moderate progress in the interests of our humanity, to mitigate the excesses of the Second Estate through moral persuasion, and to provide comfortand hope to the Third Estate.

The convolutions of the human conundrum are reaching epic and dangerous limits; they present risk, as never before, to the very fabric of human society andin the sustainability of the earth and its' ecosystems, and yet, people of high and low rank still turn to the religions of the world for, if no longer guidance, at least for a measure of reassurance, or a reference point in this seemingly unravelling world order; the world order that was secured after WW2, which order is now under insidious attack.

In anticipation of this challenging and often confusing maelstrom, the book common to every iteration of

Christianity, the Bible, promises, within itself, safe passage to those that heed its guidance. It is therefore more than ironic….it is tragic that the "babel" of voices of interpretation, the abuses of religious authority and the manipulations of the power of faith, have colluded to add to thecacophony, the dissonance, which pervades our thinking, as a society.

It is a foundational article of faith that the Judeo-Christian God, Jehovah, with whom there "is not the variation of the turning of a shadow", will provide guidance and direction commensurate with the challenges of our times. Indeed, in the words of the Psalmist, we are repeatedly exhorted to "wait for God, for I [we] shall yet laud him as the grand salvation of my [our] person, and as my [our] God".

Now, this expectation for deliverance is not built around the mystical concept of "merkabah" as a vehicle to deliver mankind. In times past, as recorded in Biblical history, deliverance has been a literal human experience, as in, the parting of the Red Sea or the conveyance of life within an ark. In each case, the method was accompanied by Divine direction, delivered by God-appointed leaders who spoke with the voice of conviction amidst an overwhelming noise of circumstance.

These clear and clarion calls to action, upon which individual lives depended, stood out from the rancorous, conflicted and often inward-gazing thoughts expressed by a cluttered and confused myriad of voices, coming from the many disciplines of thought current in each age. Such a distinct and compelling call emerged in the unique cross current of thought authored by one Charles Taze Russell in the late nineteenth century. The premise herein supported is that thecore values that were engendered in the teachings of CT Russell must re-emerge as a New World Society.

We await attendance of the Divine Being to these matters; we anticipate a clarion call in our day. A call for deliverance into a New World Order. It most assuredly will become evident "just in time".

Let the reader use discernment.

CHAPTER 3: EMANCIPATION FROM FEAR

A compelling case for the rejection of traditional Christian teaching, often cited by those of any spiritual (versus religious) ilk, is the distasteful notion that a loving God can be the inflictor of torment. History shows that accentuation of this perceived threat, promoted for dubious reason, has resulted in the subjugation of poorly educated parishioners of the Catholic Church, as one example; there are many more such examples. The fear thus inspired has been a blunt tool in leading supplicants to do the bidding of "the church".

There is a fable about motivation that I am sure most of us were told in our youth, of a contest between the sun and the wind to accomplish the removal of a certain traveller's coat. As the story goes, in a show of bravado, the wind promised that, by force, he could do the task, with the result that the coat was drawn tighter. The sun, however, was successful in inducing the desired result by a generous application of warmth. The "wind" of fear at work in those religions of Christendom (and heathendom, by the way) that carried on such manipulation was replaced, in the enlightened teachings of Russell, by a sense of trust in God as a loving Father.

Perhaps there is no single more influential factor in the attractiveness of the messaging of CTR than in his debunking of the doctrine of eternal punishment bythe God of the Bible. He is reported to have engaged in debate with any and all comers on this issue, more often than any other issue. In so doing, the traditional clergy felt clearly threatened at the loss of a cornerstone of their hold on the people, and their attendant power.

While we could also include certain Eastern religions as perpetrators, let us consider two examples within mainstream Christendom, the Catholics and theBaptists:

The Roman Catholic Church was the clever creation of Emperor Constantine, devised in order to create an illusion of a Christian foundation for a Holy Roman Empire. In truth, this move, while claimed to be one of piety, was a devious and calculated attempt to "manage" a growing Christian presence within his domain. As a skilled empire builder, the Emperor needed to placate his prior base, those who clung to pantheistic traditions and ritualistic worship of their deities, and, at the same time, accommodate Christianity. In a deft application of his political and nation-building skills, Constantine merged one into the other. He professed Christianity to seize hold of the currents of the time, and he and his newly minted church appointees decreed, for the benefit of his pagan followers, that the Christianity of the HolySee would continue to observe all pagan customs, essentially so that then the partying could go on!

Amongst other things, the Feast of Saturnalia became known as the concurrent time for the celebration of Christmas, which ostensibly celebrates the birth of Christ. The Roman Catholic Church integrated various levels of suffering, as framed in pagan lore, into doctrine, namely, limbo, purgatory and hades; all such, of course, from which one could be escaped through various indulgences, to which Luther objected, but, again, I digress. Such was the "Christianity" born of the Council of Nicea in 325 AD.

A foundational Baptist teaching is the promise of torture in eternal hellfire for unrepentant sinners, and while the Bible does use the word "hell" and, also, while there is the symbolic reference to the use of fire in the accomplishment of complete and utter eradication, nowhere does the scriptural record paint God as the author of any suffering, let alone such inhumane and unloving punishment as an endless burning of His human children in any "hell".

Let us here set aside the notion that manipulation by fear is just a religious construct, since fear has always been a primary influencer of human initiative, or lack thereof. A study of human personality, for laymen, easily researched via the Internet, is presented as the "Four Colour Personality" theory. It holds that the primary point of concern for 55% of all people is their need for security and that it is the next highest priority for about 22% more. This significant insight into humankind explains, to a large degree, why so many people throughout the centuries have been held to ransom by religious manipulations that promise "this…. if you do that", or "burn in hell…if you do this".

As an aside, it is a tragic paradox that today, in the Christian Congregation of Jehovah's Witnesses, the threat of disfellowshipping is held out in exactly the same way; it is a fear inducing prospect held over every JW.

CT Russell was able to build a substantial case for the absolute rejection of any notion of torment by the loving God, Jehovah. Rather, the God of the Bible, in the Christian scriptures, the New Testament, was demonstrably kind, compassionate and loving, as demonstrated by his emissary to mankind, Jesus Christ.

This character study, based on Holy Scripture, is, and was, the most attractive component in the ministry of Jehovah's Witnesses, as they are currently known.Many are the former Catholics, and people of varied "Christian" iterations, who have joined the ranks of the CCJW (Christian Congregation of JW's), as they have come to appreciate their God as a loving and supportive father; one who has made provision for good conscience in each of us, although not one of us isperfect; one who chooses to see the best in mankind's efforts to grow into spirituality, as opposed to a God who is always on the lookout for our stumbles, and who exacts penalty for all of our falters.

Indeed, an important scriptural reference says that he prefers to "put our sins far off, as far as east is from west", from his view of us. This is a far cry from the Catholic concept of a God who is "omnipotent, omniscient, omnipresent", and we might add, "overbearing".

These appealing new revelations about the nature of God explain the breathtaking growth of the movement started by CTR. There is tragic irony that,whilst presenting this loving God through their ministry, and thus attracting good-hearted ones with the power of God's loving personality, an organisational need to set the movement apart from established norms of mainstream Christendom led to the development of a sometimes uneasy apprehension amongst the rank and file JW's. This apprehension is in full flower today. Pleasenote, true Christians accept discipline willingly; it is just that the JW "discipline" these days seems to be a lot more like "punishment"!

CHAPTER 4: THE NUB OF THINGS

DELIVERING A NEW WORLD ORDER, as stated in our first tome, traces a sequence starting with the arrival of the greatest teacher ever to live on this goodearth.

Now, let us restate the foundation upon which this entire treatise is built: while Jesus Christ is universally seen as a significant person (even beyond Christendom) in world history; and while he is most often seen as the founder of and inspiration for a major religious body; it is our contention that Jesus Christ had no interest, whatsoever, in establishing any religion. In fact, he forswore religion, and, more to the point, he utterly rejected the religious leaders of his day.His ministry had no purpose other than to kindle a Christian set of values, and to build hope in the suffering peoples he encountered. On the other hand, those Jewish rabbis, scribes and Pharisees typified the whole gamut of religious leaders - leaders of Christendom, Islam, Mormon and all other religious systems. They all have in common a love of the power of control over their adherents, and even more, a love of the riches delivered upwards through each respective hierarchy, to them. It is a sad reality that the innate human need to reverence the Most High is channelled for vainglorious ends through each belief system. Jesus referred to the Jewish leaders of his day as "offspring of vipers", "whitewashed graves", "fine china teacups left unwashed for centuries" and a few other choice descriptors, showing his contempt for their "religiosity". Such descriptors might be applied to religious leaders that you, dear reader, have observed in your own life.

And we marvel that the movement initiated by CT

Russell in the late 19th century made such dramatic inroads into the bailiwick of Christendom. Charles Taze Russell was a social media guru a century before Mark Zuckerberg was a twinkle in his daddy's eye, and the growth of his following in just 45 years would approximate <u>a million hits in 2 days</u> on today's most voracious web postings.

And let us say here, that for critics of Russell (& Rutherford & Knorr), no-one has yet dissected the life of Mark Zuckerberg. His success as evidenced by the penetration of Facebook, worldwide, is his marker.

Having gained a constituency using the media tools of his day – his syndicated newspaper column, town hall forums, moving pictures – Russell created a business entity to promote his messages.

<u>This is a significant point worth reiteration</u>: when he incorporated the first WATCHTOWER, BIBLE AND TRACT SOCIETY in Pittsburgh PA, Russell specifically said that the WTB&TS was simply a mechanism to support a ministry; to paraphrase "<u>this corporation will not be a religion</u> in any ordinary sense of the word, ever". In imitation of his own saviour, Jesus Christ, he eschewed organised religion, with its' rites, hierarchies and opulence.

Having created a corporate structure, having financed the venture out his own funds, having expended himself by every means imaginable in disseminating a new version of Christianity which in the minds of his copious followers most closely conformed to the Christianity of the first century, Charles Taze assumed the role of President of the WTB&TS.

There followed two successors, Joseph "Judge" Rutherford and Nathan H. Knorr,before the usurpation of the movement by a newly conceptualised Governing Body. They superimposed a "rule by committee" model which, over the succeeding 50 years, gradually but unavoidably dissipated the energy amassed under the business model originally intended by the founder.

We could summarise the progression of the movement in this way:

- <u>FIRST BLUSH</u>: approximately 45 years – from conceptualization to inception, to quantum growth as 1914 approached, to incredible disappointment, to drop-off in membership, to death of Russell in 1916.

- <u>LIFE SUPPORT</u>: approximately 26 years – from near collapse to corporate reset, to renewal, to bold initiative, to rebranding during the Rutherford tenure.

- <u>A NEW AGE</u>: approximately 33 years – from recovery to stability, to worldwide expansion, to incremental growth under the leadership of Knorr. It is said of the early Christians of the first century that they were highly visible and unstoppable…under Knorr the JW's, despite their relatively small numbers, were present and active and they, too, were seemingly everywhere.

- <u>WHICH BRINGS US TO 1970's</u>: a coup of sorts takes place – a collective leadership, known as the Governing Body takes over a dynamic, seemingly unstoppable momentum and, notwithstanding continuation of growth for a few decades, presides over the dissipation of energy, allowing the now dominant <u>religious</u> entity, the

CCJW (Christian Congregation of Jehovah's Witnesses), to emulate every other religious body in this world, not in its' teachings, but, in its' hierarchical structure.

The following sequence of thought presumes that the movement, at its inception, and for most of its history, has been blessed by the Great God and guided by Jesus Christ.

We will not get caught up in revisionist questioning of character common to so many who have turned on the faith. The evidence is clear.... the contemporaneous masses responded to the magnet of "the Truth", as developed by Russell and his followers, and this is the best measure of the movement....it is a sad fact that many try to deconstruct the movement by personally diminishing its' leaders, including individual Governing Body members. It is all too easy to pick at personal flaws in others, in hindsight. Besides which, the individual members of the Governing Body have devoted lifetimes to their ministries -theirs' is a collective failure.

CHAPTER 5: ADOPTION OF THE STRUCTURE OF A RELIGION

The mission of Jesus Christ, in coming to the earth, was twofold - to ease pain and to deliver hope, the hope of a New World Order. The NWO is a subset of, a stepping stone to, the accomplishment of the original purpose of God for humankind; remember? - "fill the earth and subdue it, have it in subjection….", etc. Engendered in this phrasing is the presumption that the earth and its ecosystems were perfect to begin with; that the earth was perfectly suited to the unlimited enjoyment of life; that it was, starting with Eden, the quintessential paradise.

Now, notwithstanding where human history started, with failure, let us reflect on the evident pattern of God's dealings with humans, in furtherance of the Divine Purpose, as above: whenever something needed to happen in support of the Divine Purpose, individuals were "raised up" (read: brought to prominence), men and women, who demonstrated some unique capacity for the given task at hand. These ones, think of Moses, Miriam - Moses' sister, Mary - Jesus' "mother", Saul - later Paul, etc., became His channel for delivery of a crucial result, i.e. they were "chosen" because of their experience, their traits and, mostly, their heart quality. They were used to each deliver a step along the path to the NWO, and again, the NWO is simply an assertion of God's original purpose for life on earth.

Charles T. Russell, as evidenced by the enduring strength of his movement, and notwithstanding the abysmal condition of the CCJW at this moment, was such a man "raised up" as a bulwark against the bastardised versions of Christianity of his day. <u>He was not the first to take such a stand</u>, subsequent to the Catholic dominance. Think of William Tyndale, Christian, printer, lover of God and martyr in the cause of delivering sacred scripture to the common man. Please recognise, dear reader, Tyndale could not have been perfect, ergo neither could be Russell.

Judge Rutherford, too, demonstrated remarkable, and offensive to many, grit in the face of severe disappointment over 1914. JR was not perfect, either.

And what can we say about Nathan H. Knorr? In his short tenure, Knorr fulfilled the aspiration of the founder in building a stirring, dynamic "business" model for the dissemination of "The Good News Of The Kingdom".

Frederick Franz was an enigma, a short term President of the WTB&TS who supported Knorr as Vice-President for many years. Franz got lost in himself, and egotistically predicted 1975. Ultimately, he gave rise to the dissatisfaction which led to a Governing Body.

Knorr passed late in the 1970's, followed by Franz in the 1980's, however, long before, both were retired to less prominent roles. There had been challenges from the subset of leadership immediately below the President and VP of the WTB&TS, taking umbrage at the concentration of power and influence of the secular entity and its officers. This was an entirely predictable complication arising from the success of building the New World Society worldwide, in light of the "human factor" of ambition. Upper Management at the WTB&TS Headquarters expressed a desire to subjugate the

Body Corporate to a "rule by committee". There was also some debate about the nature of the "faithful and discreet slave" referred to by Jesus Christ at Matt. 24:45. It was a time of testingand adjustment.

I am reminded here of a plaque purchased by my mother and placed on a shelf in our family library. The quotation it bore is a play on John 3:16, known and quoted in every Christian iteration across history:

"For God so loved the world"....*HE DIDN'T SEND A COMMITTEE!*

Just as significant as the change in designation, from Society to Organization, was the notion that the dynamic movement, which had been channelled by God'smen of the moment, Russell, Rutherford and Knorr, who seized opportunity and generated immense enthusiasm, could productively morph into a committee driven model with its' attendant issues, namely, politicking, patronisation and showy religiosity.

A Governing Body was conceptualised and rationalised; the resulting convolutions cramped the heretofore efficient management structure of the WTB&TS. The transition to this new arrangement was accompanied by two key developments:

In a lapse of judgement attributable, once again, to a measure of egotism, Franz(a Rhodes Scholar) embarked on a speculative journey into Biblical references as to time and prophecy, and took it upon himself to predict 1975 as the point in time when 6,000 years of history since the creation of man would happen. The implication, based on the official position that each creative "day" was 7,000 years, was that the 1,000-year rule of Christ, the millennium, would therefore begin.

In preparation for the fulfilment of this prediction, a decision was made to introduce a new model for oversight at the local congregational level. This arrangement mirrored the move to the Governing Body (of Supreme ELDERS), thus it was called the Elder Arrangement.

The appointment of elders in each congregation, collectively known as a Body of Elders per congregation, reflected a philosophy that opened the door for all male members to strive for eldership. This adjustment essentially rewarded men for long service, as opposed to the prior arrangement where a select few were chosen to lead, based on leadership quality. The structure was an expansion of what was known as a Service Committee of three men; and whereas the prior arrangement effectuated results with a minimum of oversight necessary to coordinate the operation of each individual congregation, today, the Elder Class has become an identifiable subset of the Organization. Its' members are the "elites" in a two tiered caste system that has paralysed growth, and that has led to a top heavy model of Christianity, where service to the needs of the "sheep" is secondary to the support and preeminence of the religious structure of the elites.

This new model was "sold" as a return to the model of the Christian congregation of the first century!

Suffice it to say that there is no evidence of a permanent administrative "Governing Body" in the Bible, attached to the early Christian movement. The single reference to a senior Body of Elders, located at the birthplace of Christianity, Jerusalem, is in the context of the need for an assembly of learned and experienced voices to quell disputing between Christians of Jewish extraction, and those of Gentile extraction, over questions of Israelite law, as applied to Christianity.

One might liken the assembly of such a "council" to the practice, in Israel, for questions of the day to be adjudicated "at the city gate" by men of experience in life and the application of law; this provision existed in every city in Israel. The Jewish tradition was, and is, for open discussion of problems presented "at the gate"; this was an informal opportunity for anyone with an interest, or with relevant insight, to participate in a group discussion of problems and situations presented. An example enshrined in Israelite law saw any inadvertent manslayer offered the opportunity to flee to a designated "city of refuge" where "at the gate" his defence would be heard by older men of the city, who would confirm or deny his claim of innocence. This was no formal court, however it was a practical arrangement for dealing with questions of pressing importance.

If ever the first century council of older men of the Christian congregation in Jerusalem was re-assembled, or indeed, whether another such council was ever assembled anywhere in that first century Christian community, the Bible does not say, and certainly, while the terms "older man" and "elder" are used in the letters of Paul and others, such reference does not in any way imply a formal, titled eldership as part of a power structure. Any such suggestion would lead the earlyChristians to the practise of Christianity as a "religion", which Christianity was never intended to be.

And yet, that is exactly what the Christian Congregation of Jehovah's Witnesses has become, under the guidance and tutelage of the Governing Body.

EDITOR'S NOTE: As we prepare to go to press this October Day, new confirmation has arrived......at the annual General Meeting of the WTB&TS at World Headquarters a resolution was passed removing the need for any measurement of activity in any proselytising for congregation members. On the other hand, all members of the Organisation were reaffirmed to meet a reporting requirement of time spent in "theocratic activities".

If there were any doubt about Russell's movement having morphed into a religion, this should dispel it. Hector Warburton used to say "what makes us asociety and NOT a religion is that we have never had, and never will have, a clergy/laity distinction, as we did in Methodism". Well, Hector was wrong!

As of this date, October 7, 2023 the "clergy" of the Organisation ministers to the "laity" of the CCJW; the turning inward is now complete. It is very much like navel-gazing.... Russell, Rutherford and Knorr are turning in unison in their respective graves at this *ABOMINATION*......" line dancing from hell" might be an apt descriptor of the three former presidents, today. ;-)))))

CHAPTER 6: A FAITHFUL & DISCREET SLAVE

"Who really is the faithful and discreet slave whom his master appointedover his domestics, to give them food at the proper time?"

Matthew 24:45

This rhetorical question was raised by Jesus Christ, as part of the answer he gave to the question posed by his disciples at Matthew 24:3.

When considered in context, the question suggests a new provision, under the arrangement of Christ, for further guidance to be provided at the time of the "presence" of Christ, his second coming. An entity known as the faithful & discreet slave would be tasked with supplying (spiritual) food to the "domestics", this referring to individual Christians. This suggests an arrangement for an expanded application of Christianity, new light, if you will, on the practice of faith, specific to the time period that Jesus described in earlier verses.

Under the leadership of CT Russell, provision was made for a publishing arm to his ministry, The Watchtower Bible & Tract Society of Pennsylvania. This, and many other Watchtower Societies (including the IBSA in Britain) spread across the globe have produced an uninterrupted stream of publications which detail all aspects of "the Truth", as we know it. Credit is due for the remarkable effort and appropriate use of resources to make available far and wide that set of teachings which define "the Truth".

There have been an amazing variety of themes, all designed to enlighten Christians and to build appreciation for the many faceted jewels that these truthsfound in the Bible are.

There have been publications of all kinds, from books entitled Children, to Paradise Lost To Paradise Regained, to The Truth That Leads To Eternal Life, toWhat Does The Bible Really Teach?, to name just a few.

There have been interpretive scholarly works such as Commentary On The Book Of James, interlinear original language comparisons of scriptural texts and volumes of history such as Jehovah's Witnesses In The Divine Purpose.

There have been an equally impressive number of formats, from tracts, to brochures, to magazines, to bound volumes of the Watchtower and Awakemagazines.

It is the contention of this treatise that this cumulative evidence points to the "faithful & discreet slave" as an entity associated with the Watchtower Bible & Tract Society. This presumption is not unqualified, and it has been a subject of some debate as to who or what actually constitutes the F&DS. At the time of Knorr, the position taken was that this slave was an amorphous composite bodyof all those living on earth during the "end times" who professed to have an anointing to life in heaven.

This was termed to be a "remnant" of the 144,000 referred to in Revelation as sitting as King-Priests in heaven - associate rulers under Jesus Christ, of the Kingdom. These ones submitted their thoughts on scripture to the Watchtower Society which was, as originally intended by Russell, a repository of these submissions and, also, a tool for the distillation, printing and dissemination of truths thus derived. This understanding, and this manner of developing spiritualawareness and understanding, was consistent with Russell's style.

Now, at the time of the introduction of the Governing Body and the Elder Arrangement, there was some disputing at JW Headquarters amongst those considering the leadership structure about whether or not there was a formal process in place to engage this faithful & discreet slave in development of published materials, as reported in the book Crisis of Conscience, authored by a disbarred former Governing Body Member, Raymond Franz.

There is no question that the publications of the Watchtower Society were a comprehensive and timely source of material that furthered understanding of theDivine Purpose, nor is there any question that the Watchtower Society, by tradition, was accepting of, even solicitous of, incoming letters that provided comment on all things spiritual, nor can it be denied that the resulting books, magazines, etc. satisfied a hunger for this steady supply of spiritually stimulatingmaterial.

It is a failing of hyper-organisation that leads men to try to harness such a process; it is a failing of ego that this wonderful, communal, hazily defined process that served the early development of "the Truth" has fallen under the purview of a very few men; there has been a blurring of lines that has seen thedesignation coalesced into the Governing Body. Who do they think they are?

Their bold claim to this title was revealed in a Watchtower study article in 2013.

This centralisation of all things Watchtower into a Governing Body that has no precedent in scripture has led to the sluggish, inward looking and top heavy entity that now rules over the Christian Congregation of Jehovah's Witnesses. It has seen the GB/F&DS become entangled in matters far beyond the delivery of "spiritual food"; it has seen controversy over mishandling of very serious matters;it has led to the failure of oversight detailed in this book; it has led to a dispirited and diminishing congregation; it is a tragedy.

Where does the CCJW stand after 50 years of this Elder Arrangement?

Seemingly, the movement that started with the efforts of Charles Taze Russellhas stalled. The core teachings remain the same, their power to attract honest-hearted ones has not diminished, and yet growth is non-existent.

CHAPTER 7: FORMAL WORSHIPPERS, SUPERFINE APOSTLES

Paul himself was personally appointed as an apostle, by the resurrected Jesus Christ. Paul was the original "travelling overseer", visiting local congregations in the first century to encourage and upbuild. He was hard working, unassuming and astonishingly forthright. He remarked on the fact that his writings were sometimes perceived to be hard-nosed, while in person he was unpretentious. He supported himself, for the most part, earning his keep as a tentmaker, and heneither relied on tithed giving, nor did he exact any price from those he taught orministered to in any fashion. This was all in stark contrast to the levels of opulence which must be sustained on behalf of the religious hierarchies of the constructs of Christendom.

There are a number of references within the writings of the Apostle Paul identifying certain specific types of Christian persona. Now, even though no formal power structure was in place in the Christianity of his day, there clearlywere troubling trends in the way that membership developed as those early Christian communities developed. There are certain tendencies that emerge within the human psyche within any social structure; such were present in the congregations within which Paul served, and upon which he reflected in his letters. We read Paul's references to "formal worshippers" and "superfine apostles" with great interest.

It must be said that the vast majority of those who have been attracted to the teachings of Jehovah's Witnesses, are by nature humble and unassuming. They emulate Paul in their diligence and in their integrity. However, with the growing emphasis on the importance of organisational considerations within the CCJW, certain traits have come to the forefront, especially in the Elder Class. If formal worshippers and superfine apostles emerged in a loosely arranged congregation in Paul's day, how likely is it that, with inordinate importance placed on religious structure, the Witnesses would fall victim in a similar way? One need only look at the more egregious examples in the worldwide religionhood, across all faiths, where pride, prominence and pomposity count far more than piety, or spirituality, for an answer.

So, there is nothing wrong with "formal" worship, even if the practice of true Christianity is more organic, lived at the level of daily life. Even if CT Russell and his followers eschewed any kind of formality in favour of peer-to-peer discussion, but if Paul was inspired to point out this specific category of early Christians, it must be that, from the weight of emphasis alone, such formality displayed as unbalanced.

Similarly, the "superfine" is a derivative of the word "fine" and thus implies fine-ness taken to an extreme. We must remember that while communities of Christians did, and do associate together for mutual encouragement, the exercise of Christianity is very much an individual undertaking - as with snowflakes, no two Christians, or Christian consciences, are the same. Each adherent builds the application of Christianity according to his or her unique experience and circumstance, according to their level of knowledge of the Christian "way", according to the mechanism of conscience to guide his or her worship, his or her choices in life, his or her conduct.

There are limits to the influence that formal worshippers and superfine apostles should try to exert on the conscientious exercise of Christianity by others. Both types glory in their position and prominence within the Christian firmament; such types are the "millers of the grist" of the human body politic; you can see them in every community of persons, religious, political, etc.

With the evolution of Russell's movement into a religion, with the attainment of eldership in increasing numbers (in some congregations of the JW's today, especially in the western world, elders number 50% or more of the male constituency), with the relative malaise in recruitment of new converts, the proliferation of the formal and the superfine within the ranks of the Elder Class (includes all of local elders, travelling elders and those within the Organization's network of branch and headquarters facilities), has led to a top heavy and overbearing practice of oversight.

Requirements for qualification for appointment as an elder have gone beyond scriptural standards. Loyalty to an organisation is exaggerated. It is as if the moreformal, the more superfine, the better.

This is all suffocating to the free, open and personal exercise of Christianity. Certainly, as one who remembers well the contagious enthusiasm, the spontaneity, the joy of working within the congregation in earlier days; as one who appreciated the diversity which came from the sharing of individual goals, challenges and accomplishments, as opposed to decreed organisational objectives; I have witnessed a wilting in long time adherents (not simply attributable to old age), who have tired of the ceaseless reminders to "keep up with the "Organisation", and it is current reality that there is a discernible drop off, as measured by both activity and results in the public preaching work for which the JW's are best known.

The financial requirements of this bureaucracy, along with the burden of supporting the brick & mortar facilities of the Organisation, amount to a taxation on adherents. CT Russell was famously quoted as saying words to the effect that"when the money runs out, we'll know it's time to quit". The Governing Body can't even take a hint, they just ask for more, and more, and more.

CHAPTER 8: FALSE EXPECTATIONS RE: THE ELDER CLASS

The prophet Isaiah was inspired to speak of the coming New World Order. His descriptions of peaceful and secure conditions, as originally intended by the creator, are an inspiring and hope-inducing part of the Biblical record.

In Israel, the rule of King Solomon was the Camelot era, therefore, all successiveiterations of the exercise of rulership were measured against this period.

Solomon reigned for 70 years, and during his reign, peace and prosperity (and love) prevailed.

Isaiah uses many symbolisms to broaden our understanding of what true peace might feel like - "the lion lays down with the lamb", "the young child plays with the poisonous snake, without harm", "no-one shall foreclose on the lowly", "we sat in the shade of our trees and we enjoyed peace, and we loved".

In a larger application of the idyllic days of King Solomon, Isaiah was inspired to speak of a time when his God, Jehovah, would set about to restore peace to this planet. Perhaps in a feudal allegory to the reign of King Solomon, Isaiah wrote prophetically of a time when "princes" would arise on behalf of a new king. This king is none other than Jesus Christ, who promised to return to us at a future time, when speaking during his earthly sojourn. The arrival of princes, of which Isaiah wrote, was to be associated with the Lord's return, as King of his Kingdom, aka the New World Order.

The identity of these princes has been a mystery within the movement of Russell. History records that Rutherford conjured up expectations about their imminent arrival. There is evidence that he purchased and furnished a retreat in California in anticipation of this hoped-for eventuality. His expectation was focused on the return of ancient servants of God: Moses, Isaiah and such, via the resurrection promised for faithful pre-Christian servants of God. Truth is, he was disappointed, once again, due to some fanciful thinking, and we countenance no objection, whatsoever, to those who dream of better days and the fulfilment of all God's promises. Indeed, while we cannot predict the future, or even the timing of events prophesied in the Bible, it is a constructive use of our imaginations to project ourselves into the future that Jehovah God has in store for us.

In the workup of the Elder Arrangement, some thought that perhaps it might be alright to say that the future princes would arise from the ranks of elders. So, they reasoned, if we presume that we have found the right model, and if we sell the model, and if 1975 is the tipping point for transition from an old to a new system of things, then it must follow.....the princes of Isaiah are elders, or elders are princes in the making, or, or, or....We must remember that, on the occasion of selecting David as King, scripture reminds us that God sees beyond what mansees; an appointment as elder is no guarantee of princehood.

Such reasoning, developed in the short run-up to the predicted "end", as per Fred Franz, has proven to be debilitating; and, just as one could not deny the damage accruing from the pronouncement of "1975", the notion that appointed elders are "princes" is a thought to be held in infamy.

It would not have been so bad had the end come in 1975 when there was still only a representative number of elders. Today there are a myriad of men who secretly, or even publicly, and proudly, see themselves as princes. Even those elders for whom I still hold great respect, and affection, those who try to "serve"the needs of the "sheep" under their care, are locked into a code that says, we are presumed to be future princes of the future New World Order and, to uphold the collective body of elders, we must show solidarity to each other, first and foremost   and then we can care for our wards.

This thinking has proven to be paralysing to the CCJW: in regard to matters of conscience which arise within a congregational setting, pity the poor elder who conscientiously dissents from the democratic decision of the Body of Elders, forhe must keep his peace, back down from the dictates of his conscience, as onemust do in any political entity, as in any business management structure.

Isaiah states, in regard to those princes that they will "rule for justice itself". A preoccupation with justice does not burden the collective Elder Body of the CCJW, including the Governing Body. Their preoccupation is with their own position within an Organisation that operates in much the same way as any otherreligious or secular movement.

The presentation to the Court of the Grand Theocrat detailed in Chapter 23 is a damning testimony to the failure of the collective Body of Elders of the Christian

Congregation of Jehovah's Witnesses.

CHAPTER 9: A CULT OF ORGANISATION

As I hope we have established, the exercising of the personal practise of Christianity, even within a community of believers, suffers when the structure of religion is superimposed. A certain arbitrariness sets in when natural expression of worship is supplanted by organisational considerations.

In this sense, we might see the example of the Roman Catholic Church in the Middle Ages as the worst of excesses. During this age, a Court of Star Chamber travelled the Catholic world in pursuit of heresy against the Church. The basis for judgement of any Christian who acted on conscience was not Biblical principle but, rather, conformity to official policy. Many are the principled men who burned at the stake, or lost a head, for following their convictions. Sir Thomas Moore, memorialised in the film A Man For All Seasons, comes to mind in this regard, for his persecution and death were church sponsored. In this case, it was the Church of England, accommodating the savagery of Henry VIII in the treatment of his wives.

When the mechanics of religion take precedence over scriptural principle, a line is crossed that we can characterise as a form of idolatry.

Idolatry, literally, is defined as "excessive or blind adoration, reverence, devotion…"; it is spoken of in the Bible, first of all, in regard to the use of idols in worship. Beyond this simple manifestation, the Bible proffers the thought that anything, animate or inanimate, for which a human might form a worshipful attachment might constitute idolatry. For example, Paul states that those who indulge in excessive eating, to a point of preoccupation, might be guilty of makingtheir "bellies" a "god".

In the case of the Roman Catholic Church, we might say that Catholic adherents, in ignoring the travesty of the Court of Star Chamber, and the many other mechanisms used to inflict Catholic culture on groups as diverse as First Nations people and young Irish women, demonstrate a cult-like appearance when they continue to worshipfully bow down to, or follow direction of, a hierarchy, including the Pope, that manifestly goes against the respect due to such groups. You don't have to swallow Kool-aid to prove irrational, conscienceless devotion.

In the same way, the preoccupation that has overtaken the followers of CT Russell, 3 generations removed, qualifies Jehovah's Witnesses as a cult (with a multi headed Pope). They are a cult of the Organisation, subject to the unquestioned and unquestionable decrees of the Governing Body.

Many years ago, in an adjustment of the vow of dedication, candidates for baptism were asked, not simply to dedicate their lives to God and to ask for acceptance on the basis of Jesus' ransom sacrifice. They were asked to include the Organisation by vowing allegiance to that body. **THIS SIGNALLED THE POINT AT WHICH THIS NOBLE MOVEMENT BECAME A CULT!**

This development has taken on a life of its' own: worship of, or, at least, a worshipful attitude towards all of the Organisation, the Governing Body, Elders, permeates the mindset of all rank and file JW's - elders are tasked with ensuring that the Organisation, its' continued success, its' perpetuation, is given prominent consideration in all congregational decisions and actions

When, for instance, a problem arises between congregation members, more often than not, rather than follow the directive of Christ, as at Matthew 18:15-17, the parties are asked to make quasi-peace to keep the congregation free from controversy. The peace that is preserved is that of elders who choose not to exertthemselves as part of the adjudication process.

This imposed pseudo-peace, along with the regimentation that has, to all intents and purposes, undermined this once dynamic movement, has resulted in loss of drive, loss of enthusiasm; it has led to its' becoming a shadow of what it once was.

Even more alarming, and more serious, recently it was reported to me that, as part of a Governing Body sponsored meeting in late September of 2023, the thought was expressed that Jehovah's Witnesses are "citizens of the Organisation". What? Surely all Christians aspire to be citizens of the Kingdomof Jesus Christ. This is staggering!

It has long been held that the United Nations places itself in the rightful place of Christ's Kingdom; that the UN is usurping the authority of the King Christ Jesus. Surely, to demand fealty to an organisation that was intended to support the "great cloud of witnesses" can be classified as **_BLASPHEMY_** against the Arrangement of God. It is a total misunderstanding of the role of the "faithful & discreet slave", which entity is appointed to <u>serve</u>, not rule over, the "domestics".

CHAPTER 10: WHAT'S IN A NAME, ANYWAY?

Every person is assigned a name (although, today we might sometimes "feel like a number", t-u BOB SEGER). Corporations take great pain to establish a "brand", aka their name, their reputation. Indeed, every entity, including entities in the spiritual (religious) realm, is either assigned or develops a name, or an identity, which delivers to us a message as to who they are and what they do.

At his Town Halls, Russell took on the big names – Baptists, Catholics, Pentecostals – with no pretension; it was just Russell vs. any and all comers, of any religious ilk. Naturally, this was to his advantage, at first, because he had no record to defend, ergo, he could attack the myriad contradictions, anomalies and the sometimes stupidity evident in every religion. Although his debate opponents arrived with strong conviction, it was always more or less dispensed from above, not from heaven, but, from the pinnacle of the religion's hierarchy, e.g. the catechism upon which Catholic faith is built, unlike the Holy Scriptures, was developed subsequent to the Council of Nicea in 325 A.D. and has significant flaws, which Russell was able to exploit. However, CTR's following soon became easily identifiable as an entity, a critical mass of persons who, by the power of attraction alone, came to bear the name RUSSELLITES.

Russell himself was a modest man (though not, apparently, all that humble). As previously stated, he had no pretension about forming another religion. Indeed, it was the very religiosity manifest in those he debated that won him his following. Russell was probably flattered at the assignment of his name to the movement, but no formalised religion was intended or implemented under this banner.

A second way in which any movement or social grouping might be characterised, besides co-opting the name of its' leader, is to use a descriptor based on what the movement stands for. Under this dynamic the movement came to be known as the MILLENNIAL DAWNISTS. This moniker was a reference to the time sensitive nature of Russell's message. The urgency with which he went about his business was predicated on his dire predictions regarding the year 1914. Russell was convinced that the world as he knew it would end in 1914 and the millennium of Christ's Kingdom reign would commence. This also explains why Russell drove himself to an early death in 1916. Again, this was not a name of Russell's choosing.

Next, and this time with his approval, the name INTERNATIONAL BIBLE STUDENTS was adopted. This was more a reflection of the style of association that he intended, and while it is true that he was the spiritual leader, the President and the author of myriad books, brochures, leaflets and such, the flavour of his ministry was to attract like-minded persons into a community where each and every person made a contribution to the development of understanding of the Bible and any resulting system of belief. The meetings of naturally occurring local groupings of his adherents were not held in any church. Far from it, as with the early Christians of the first century, meetings were held informally, in private homes.

So, what, exactly, is in a name?

The Bible clarifies here; and for the sake of precision, I quote Ecclesiastes 7:1 from the *International Children's Bible*:

It is better to have respect than good perfume. The day a person dies is better than the day he was born.

Please, bear with me. We are each given a name at birth. The name we are given is an expression of hope. If well chosen, it is a predictor of who we might become, but no mother can anticipate all of the curves, opportunities or missiles that we might encounter in our lives and which strongly influence what our namewill come to mean. Hence, when we die we are better because, having run our course, there is no doubt, whatsoever, about who we have proven to be. Now, the caveat here is that no sane, balanced individual wants to die. Also, if our life has proven us to be a scoundrel or such, well, enough said. If we have lived up to our well-chosen name, despite every obstacle thrown our way, then, in this sense only, the day of our death is better than the day of our birth.

Now, how does the value of a name apply to a business, or other entity?Excellent question for you thinking people.

Well, business corporations, when they start out assign themselves a name, a brand; each company has a Business Plan, a projection of who they want to be,how they will produce, how much money they will make and, most importantly, what impression they will make on customers. This last consideration is the lifeblood of any business and determines all other dimensions of the plan. Of course, seldom, if ever, does a company's results conform exactly to the first Business Plan, and the limitation of this analogy is that a company lifespan does not correspond with a human lifespan. Some companies don't live long enough to "make a name" for themselves, but for those that last, their brand grows in measurable value – it is called "goodwill". When a business delivers value to its'customers, the government, in my case the Canada Revenue Agency, recognizes, for tax purposes, that goodwill is the true measure of the success of any business because it means that the business has earned the trust of its' customer base. Any such business will never die! It will be passed from generation to generation, from investor to investor, forever even, perhaps.

The same logic applies to spiritual (religious) entities. Each is rooted in a belief system designed to benefit its adherents (customers). The "proof is in the pudding", however, as they say, and what is the track record of mainstream religion, of any brand? Must I answer the question for you? Particularly the denominations of Christendom, because they purport to follow Christ, have each, respectively, experienced diminution of their brand value. It is true that the so-called Christian iterations are trying to buy back value by pandering to every aberrant behaviour, claiming that "anything goes" because Jesus Christ showed superlative love in all his dealings. Many practices, however, that are tolerated byChristendom, even promoted by them, are clearly condemned in inspired scripture. Must I cite examples? I don't think so, if you have studied Christian writings, such as those of the Apostle Paul. Paul was hand chosen by Christ, andwas inspired by God's holy spirit to pen what he did; Paul was persecuted from within and without the congregation for his forthrightness in these matters.

So, Russell had the advantage, as the "new kid on the block" – he had no record to defend, and he had a plethora of hypocrisy, manipulation and pagan influenced teachings of his so-called Christian debaters. In so proceeding, Russell built "goodwill" and "brand value" rapidly. He had researched church doctrine for all players, dug into the Bible intensively, listened to, and in some cases partnered with, other "new age" preachers and, most importantly, he possessed superlative oratorical skills, and a deep conviction that his was God's work.

So, back to the international Bible Students, the self-chosen moniker for the Russellites/Millennial Dawnists. Technically, the IBS still exists. You will recall that when Rutherford forced his succession as President on his fellow committee members, the group imploded. There was a breaking away, and a certain factiontook the IBS identity with them. This group still meets in homes across North America. They are a benign bunch, and they still discuss scripture, endlessly;they have no formal proselytising, no enforceable standards.

Russell's successor, Rutherford, was perceived by many to be a willful, hard driving, hard living man, and there was never any doubt that he was a leader, an Alpha male, and just the right Man of God to save the IBS movement. In masterminding its' rebirth, he offended many, and, without ever having met the man, I can assure you, dear reader, that he cared not one whit who he drove away. He was the "winnower" at a critical time. He was one of seven, incarcerated over the stand taken of neutrality during the first world war, which many viewed as unpatriotic at best, subversive, at worst. In the southern U.S., IBS members were tarred & feathered, raped, looted and murdered. Eventually exonerated of all charges, Rutherford "hit the bricks" to fulfil the mandate he worked so hard to obtain, as WTB&TS President. We marvel at how Jehovah God raises up "men of the moment" with just the right qualifications and at just the right time. Think of Moses, Nehemiah, David, Solomon, Saul (Paul) – all men who filled a need at a critical time in the outworking of the purpose of God, and, as an aside for those who point fingers at Rutherford's fondness for "tippling", part of his larger-than-life persona, we must recognize that Saul of Tarsus was much mistrusted when assigned by Christ to take up the Christian ministry. His bold, forthright letters and larger-than-life persona, infused with the confidence of receiving a calling directly from the resurrected Jesus Christ, stirred up great resentment amongst those he admonished. As even Christ experienced, speaking God's truth can be like running a gauntlet - it proved to be a life-ending gauntlet for him.

Now, the strategist always, Rutherford scheduled many a convention, published many a book, wrote more than a few himself, and generally dazzled the base, the remaining relatively few. It matters not that none of his prognostications came true; it matters not that his writing, compared to Russell's, was abysmal. What matters most, apart from the very survival of the movement, was the master stroke of marketing that set the stage for expansion under his eventual successor, Nathan H. Knorr, as follows.

The group needed a new name, a dynamic name. I take the liberty of intuitively re-constructing his thought process, as follows, 1) we are the only Christians who use God's name often and early in every conversation, and 2) we are the very best known preachers and door knockers, of the message of Jesus Christ, and 3) why not call ourselves Jehovah's witnesses? Now, it is not wrong to form a thought and, THEREAFTER, proceed to try to find scriptural justification. After all, this was what the movement was all about – the discovery and developmentof new and better ways of understanding scripture, of thinking outside the centuries old box of Christendom.

So, at a landmark convention held at **Columbus, Ohio** on **July 31, 1931** Rutherford delivered the keynote address **The Kingdom, the Hope of the World**, where he presented the plain, simple, straightforward truth that drives the ministry of Russell's followers, including Jehovah's Witnesses today: the Kingdom is a literal government, heaven based, with Jesus Christ as its' head, its' King, and by which mankind can fulfil Adam's commission, to "fill the earth and subdue it" and where, concomitantly, the balance of all earth's ecosystems will be restored to perfection. The human experience is the foremost ecosystem and, therefore, we, as humankind, will similarly be restored to equilibrium and resulting perfection.

On the very same day, Rutherford, with the bravado of a toreador, the mystery of a genie and with all the oratorical force he could muster, delivered a further address entitled **A NEW NAME** which was climaxed by the declaration: "We desire to be known as and called by the name, to wit,

Jehovah's witnesses." A resolution had been prepared and, in virtual unanimity, was passed. Well, this inspiration of marketing lit a fuse that carried the movement skyward for pretty much the rest of the century. It qualifies as a major milestone in the history of the movement and was certainly the primary marker of Rutherford's presidency.

There are a couple of things to think about here. The first, at first glance, seems trivial: the "w" in witnesses was not capitalised, but soon thereafter it would be. The second is, there was no suggestion that this title was destined to become thebrand of the movement. This is important. As presented in the resolution "Jehovah's witnesses" was a descriptor, not a title. The brand of the movement, remember, had already been established as the Watchtower Bible & Tract Society, and, notwithstanding the 1914 disappointment, the brand had weathered more than a few storms and was a trusted source of spiritual guidance for many. It had also maintained the strict partition from religion that Russell had intended. This, by the way, would prove to be an incredibly fine line to walk: to be a repository and purveyor of Christian truth without slipping into the tainted religiosity of other so-called Christian brands, or institutions, or denominations.

Sadly, the line has been crossed, over time, and today, the justification for this series of books is to provide rationale for a readjustment, a realignment withGod's purpose, as expressed through CT Russell.

To summarise: a name is important, whether a personal, a professional, a business or a religious name, and there is high potential value in a name. It at once defines us, it holds promise over time of increased worth and it is, without a doubt, our most valuable asset. Upon a good name we can build all manner of wealth, we can pass along the inheritance of our good name to our children and we can define our personal experience on its' strength.

There is one caveat here, though: if you skip back to earlier in this chapter, please note that a mother must be prescient in choosing a name. I have always marvelled that, when a woman exercises her privilege of knowing the child in her womb for 9 months before anyone else gets so much as a peek, some mothers can select a name that epitomises who they already know the child to be. If a child is mis-named, however, it can sow confusion and can work against the development of the child's potential. Stay tuned, dear reader, because this caveat will come into play as the history of the movement unfolds. <u>Note, again, Rutherford's resolution used the term and punctuation "Jehovah's witnesses", not Jehovah's Witnesses</u>.

CHAPTER 11: SECULAR CHRISTIANITY - A WAY OF LIFE

In order to understand the implications of this new name, we must recognize its origin. This new handle on the movement, clearly, was a stroke of brilliance, and Rutherford was a "big picture guy". In fact, in conceptualising, implementing and, yes, selling the new name, Rutherford was killing two birds with one stone. On the one hand, he had succeeded in stabilising the base and now needed to light a fuse that would see the zealous ones self-identify; on the other hand, Rutherford was bothered by "churchy" types that seemed juxtaposed to his personal dynamism and he had no reservation if, in reigniting the movement, he "blew them away", as we say today. At least, he needed to reach out with a persona that attracted pro-active participants as in the pre-1914 days - the ones who stood outside churches on Sunday mornings, holding "Religion is a Racket and a Snare" signs.

Now, the word "religion" must be considered here. The newly branded Jw's could still not be called a religion; in fact, Rutherford's initiative here reinforced the notion that this grouping of Christians existed for the primary reason of bearing witness to the incoming Kingdom. The phrase "bear witness" is synonymous, more or less, with the phrase "deliver testimony". This is one essential sense of what it means to "follow in the footsteps of the Christ", although this term does not solely apply to Christian proselytising - following Christ also means adoption of a set of priorities that define a way of life.

Consider further, the term "religious" does not necessarily imply participation in any religion; I reference here Dictionary.com, where religious, amongst other valid meanings, is said to mean: <u>scrupulously faithful; conscientious</u>. Rutherford's thrust was to impose a standard, or, more precisely, an aspiration, upon all those who associated with this group. All must be willing to witness, to preach, to proselytise! The newly defined "witnesses" were to be scrupulously faithful, conscientious about disseminating the "good news of the kingdom", just as first century Christians did.

When we use the descriptor "secular" to describe Christianity, it is as opposed to "religious" in a second sense of that word. Again we turn to Dictionary.com for a second shade of meaning: <u>pertaining to or connected with a monastic or religious order</u>.

So, **secular Christianity** is,

1) bereft of the showy religiosity present in most denominations, Protestant and Catholic (some more ritualistic and pompous than others),

2) aligned with the disdain for such religiosity as expressed by Christ, in scripture, and as manifest in CT Russell,

3) consistent with the reality that during the first three centuries after Christ's death, Christian communities appeared throughout the known world requiring no power hierarchy, and,

4) marked by the dominant trait of sharing - sharing

materially out of concern for mutual well-being, often, and, even more importantly, sharing of the "good news" about Jesus Christ and the coming Kingdom (aka THE NEW WORLD ORDER) with the uninformed.

Now, to address a couple of scriptural references to this new descriptor "witness", as adopted upon presentation of Rutherford's resolution - one from the Hebrew scriptures (known to some as the Old Testament) and one from the Greek scriptures (aka the New Testament).

There two biblical passages that specifically refer to "witnesses", quoted here from YOUNG's Literal Translation:

Isaiah 43:10 - Ye [are] My witnesses, an affirmation of Jehovah, And My servant whom I have chosen, So that ye know and give credence to Me, And understand that I [am] He, Before Me there was no God formed, And after Me there is none.

Hebrews 12:1 - Therefore, we also having so great a cloud of witnesses set around us, every weight having put off, and the closely besetting sin, through endurance may we run the contest that is set before us,

In neither Isaiah nor Hebrews is the word "witnesses" capitalised!

The truth is that the very first time "witnesses" appeared as "Witnesses", as in Jehovah's Witnesses, a line was crossed, a line drawn by the founder, acting according to his God-ordained mission. It is not the first time in history that an error of punctuation has changed the course of events -

think of a rock strategically placed on a railway track, a wrong turn taken late at night on an arduous journey, or a decision taken by a young person, bullishly thinking that good advice can be ignored, that must be corrected many years later.

Perhaps the capitalization of a "W" was inadvertent; whether or not, the complexion of the movement changed. This did not become apparent immediately. It took many decades and many decisions by the JW leaders, decisions undertaken on a false sense of what the name meant.

Now, in a parallel vein, there was another name, a title, secular rather than religious, that was adopted and in general use at the time of the passage of Rutherford's resolution. The followers of Russell, the International Bible Students referred, informally, to their world view as "the Truth ", and, over time, they came to refer to an entity known as "the Society". The Society came to have a double meaning: when referring to the publishing entity, the Watchtower Bible & Tract Society (WTB&TS), established by Russell, "the Society" was a colloquial reference to the corporation which was the source of written material promoting the spiritual thinking associated with "the Truth", that set of beliefs parsed by Russell and his associates, which differentiated all his followers from the adherents of Christendom - and by osmosis, it seems, "the Society" also came to describe the "great cloud of witnesses" as a "New World Society".

The New World Society was attractively juxtaposed to the religions of Christendom. The NWS made no claim to being a religion. It was memorialised twice in the 1950's by production of moving pictures produced by the WTB&TS,

entitled "The New World Society at Work " and "The Happiness of the New World Society ". These films portrayed a society of people, united in purpose, serving together as brothers-in-arms, joyful and motivated in their ministry and service to, not Knorr, not Rutherford, not Russell (and, certainly, not to any Governing Body), but, to their saviour, Jesus Christ, and to the Great God, Jehovah.

Now, we will leave it up to the reader to intuit the ascendency of the designation JW over NWS; it doubtless migrated over time. Both were used simultaneously for some time, and the migration had to do with presumptions about the practise of religion which many converts brought with them to the movement. Most influential would be the presence, within the movement, of two categories of Christians identified by the Apostle Paul as "formal worshippers" and "superfine apostles" - these were the bane of Paul's existence and inspired his efforts, evident in his letters, to maintain the authenticity of true Christianity. His letters were a bulwark against the ritualism, power mongering and pretentious religiosity that has burdened every iteration of Christendom.

And finally, within the corrupted version of the New World Society known as Jehovah's Witnesses, under the auspices of a Governing Body, which sits atop this once liberating movement, power mongering, manipulation, control and pretentiousness have enveloped Russell's movement, too.

As possibly the best proof of this, this book, in manuscript form, was provided to the lawyers for the WTB&TS, both here in Canada and at Patterson, NY, prior to publication.

It is clear from the non-response to an offer of open discussion, with a view to a return to the values of the first three Presidents, that the Governing Body is content with the status quo.

CHAPTER 12: GENERATIONAL SLIPPAGE

It is odd, don't you think, that a protest movement such as CT Russell initiated, a refreshing departure from Christendom, would morph into a mirror image of the institutions which make up that body? While the core teachings of "the Truth" have such liberating effect, the superstructure of religion built up around it ultimately suffocates its' freeing power; when conformity and protection of the hierarchy take highest precedence, the jewel of "the Truth" becomes tarnished, corrupted.

I speak with conviction here. As a third generation follower of CTR, a person raised in the culture of the JW's, I have the advantage of knowing the mindset of my grandparents, among the early converts to the movement. I think in particular of Hector Curtis Warburton, my paternal grandfather.

Hector was an eccentric man, at first glance, short, with an elfish smile, a WW1 veteran (evidenced by the gouge taken out of his head by a lodged bullet, removed to leave an elliptical notch on his scalp, 2 to 3 inches long and half an inch deep - all the more obvious due to his bald pate), and Hector was, if anything, engaging, to those he encountered in his Christian ministry. He was humble, if not modest. To his family, his children, his grandchildren, including me, he was remote.

Hector pursued the most pacifist of occupations in his dotage, when I knew him. He was an avid gardener, in the English tradition, and I was told of recognition he received, at county fairs, each fall, for his record setting yield per pound of seed potato, for his harvest. He cultivated anything that would grow in those cool, damp English summers, including celery. My own recollection, on an occasion when I visited, was of a true Brit, rubber boots (wellies), rubber gloves, with spade in hand, dressed to the nines - jaunty cap, dress shirt and tie, woollen vest - working at his pride, his garden. We spoke little, tho' he tried to give me a few gardening tips ....just what a ten year old needed….I was soon off on my bike.

Hector also had a love of music. He made an adequate living for his family of seven by engaging both of these talents. He hired himself out as a gardener, he taught piano and he occupied the privileged position of organist at the Methodist church in Cleethorpes, Lancashire, which was a paid position.

I am certain that his most outstanding quality was courage, especially as manifest in his willingness to speak boldly and with conviction about his faith, anywhere to anyone.

Surely, such courage, born of fear, as courage always is, must have been forged in the recovery rooms of the First World War, engulfed as he must have been, in pain and fear, fear for his very life.

Now, just because he had a titled, paid position at the Methodist church, a position which surely made him conspicuous within that small community, did not mean that he, like many do, would settle for the placebo of Christianity known as Methodism.

Methodism is only one of many subsets of Christendom - the commonality of belief within the schisms of Christendom is astounding, but qualified, in each case, with curious eccentricities of organisation or tangential teaching, but I digress.

When exposed to the liberating writings of Russell and Rutherford, there was no hesitation - Hector resigned his commission as organist and wrote a letter of withdrawal from the church. This cost him, not only his due as organist - he lost many of his customers, too. The privation thus incurred was borne by his entire family, resulting in relocation and an immense adjustment of lifestyle.

More than this, Hector's fervency in response to these new teachings was such that he undertook to devote a significant portion of his time to "spreading the word" as a fulltime "pioneer", in those days a very demanding proposition. When I knew him, decades later, he had served continuously in this style of life. Eccentricities aside, Hector struck all who encountered him, outside his family, as the quintessentially dedicated, principled and prolific witness to Jehovah God that he surely was.

Hector typified all of those early witnesses to the truth-telling of the New World Society (NWS). His commitment was as Paul exhorted the early Christians, "We desire each one of you to show the same industriousness so as to have the full assurance of the hope down to the end......". More than this, that emerging community was bound together by a camaraderie of liberation that emanated from the heart. The teachings of Jesus Christ liberated Israel from a stultifying, suffocating system of worship; the extrapolations of the

NWS did so for true followers of Christ. Both Russell and Christ touched hearts, not just minds, hence the evangelistic fervour evident in HC Warburton and his contemporaries. There was also a liberation from the hierarchical structures that had been built into the Christianity of Christendom. These early proselytisers of the NWS served shoulder to shoulder, in spreading the "good news of the kingdom"; it was magical and motivating, I am sure.

At this point, we must make clear that any movement, to accomplish anything, must be corralled and directed. My choice of words here is key to our treatise. One might be tempted to use the word "organised"; "coordinated" is my word of choice. Remember, dear reader, that the founder of the modern day iteration of "true" Christianity, CT Russell, had specified that at no time would his Watchtower Society be mistaken for a "religion"; "organisation" is a euphemism for "control" in its' religious application, as proof of this, the most obvious proof, Constantine organised the state religion of Rome to control the Christian movement of his day. He did not coordinate; "to coordinate" lacks the control implied in "to organize".

And so, even though the leaders of the movement started by Russell did set up a structure, it was a structure for coordination, and it coordinated a society, a dynamic, an individually self- motivated grouping of aspirants driven solely by heart appreciation.

Sadly, it has come to be known as an organisation, with all of the implications herein discussed. As a point of note: nowhere in the sacred scriptures will you find the word "organise" or any of its derivatives.

On the subject of "organisation", let us follow another sequence of thought that is germane to this discussion. Organisations are formed by humans - in business, in government, in the arts, in the charitable world, everywhere, to address specific goals. Organisation is a human necessity, and the value of such structures cannot be overstated, in the march towards progress in any field, and yet, the Bible refers to God as a "God of order", not as a "God of organisation". Why?

Well, you have probably noticed that, in the wider world, beyond human structures, there is a self-sustaining order that, left alone, would support an infinite existence of the world, the earth, the ecosystem, that is our home, and you have probably also noticed that, notwithstanding the good accomplished by manmade organisations in pursuit of their respective goals, there are usually, if not always, unanticipated outcomes resulting from human progress. Need I give an example? OK, think about the invention of plastic, a scientific breakthrough with immense application which is now permeating land, sea and air, to our detriment…enough said.

This is a fine point, but not too fine. While the early adherents, who eventually became known as JW's, served together out of goodwill and as brothers, and accepted the evident need for coordination and direction, there came to be a false notion in regard the Organization (capitalised for much the same reason that "witness" evolved into "Witness"), arising from a well-intentioned resolution presented by Rutherford in 1931. And, like any organisation constructed and operated by humans, there have been unintended consequences.

Herein is the generational failure of the Governing Body and its band of loyalists who have presumed to "run the show"; those who have evolved the structure which developed most extensively under the leadership of N.H. Knorr and who have presumptuously installed themselves as a multi headed Pope. Over their tenure, we have seen slowing growth of the NWS/CCJW movement; in so doing, they have effectively deferred the accomplishment of God's purpose.

There is little wonder that Jesus Christ himself, in pointing to a "faithful and discreet slave" (a title which the Governing Body has commandeered) tasked with coordinating and growing Kingdom interests in this "time of the end", suggested the eventuality that <u>what was once "faithful and discreet" might be found to be "evil"</u>.

CHAPTER 13: FAILURE OF OVERSIGHT

Let us envision Russell's movement to be an ark, a sailing vessel commissioned for the preservation of life. This is no obtuse idea, as the scriptures speak of "that which corresponds to this", the "this" being the ark which Noah was commissioned to build; and according to contextual comment in the writings of the Apostle Peter, the "that" being the life-preserving arrangement for survival from an Old World Order to a New World Order in our time, the "time of the end".

Noah's ark took an estimated 80 - 90 years to construct, as he divided his time between building and preaching the end, as the world of his time knew it. The ark of salvation for us today was started, shall we say, starting at or around 1870, when Russell was commissioned to commence the foundation, the hull, of another ark, a time period of about 160 years. Considering the scale, 8 persons (and the genetic code of all earthly life) compared to the 8 million currently aboard, the 80 million likely to board, and the potentiality of many more, we are on a reasonable timeline, our trajectory being thus determined at "godspeed".

So, what happened structurally? We considered in our previous chapter the vicissitudes at play in the minds and hearts of the "great cloud of witnesses". Now let us put our minds to structural matters.

Here we must re-introduce Nathan H. Knorr. In volume 1, I described Nathan as a superlative "sales manager". In the world around him, halcyon times were at hand, the world moved into a new order subsequent to the vanquishment of the axis forces and liberty and opportunity were latent and about to explode. Nathan Knorr was a man for this time. Rutherford had stemmed the tide, turned things around and planted a seed of ennoblement in the heretofore stumbling movement. Nathan Knorr was positioned to "take the reins", to build momentum, and he did.

To compare the structure of Jehovah's Witnesses at this moment in their history to an emerging sales organisation would be trite, nevertheless, there were commonalities. Knorr built an impressive, worldwide organisation dedicated to the efficient dissemination of the "good news of the Kingdom".

Knorr put in place a structure of oversight. The purpose was, firstly, to efficiently deliver the prodigious publishing initiatives of the WTB&TS. As with any sales force (which the JW's were not, in the literal sense), the dynamics of motivation and technique bore most attention. A network of coordination was put in place - each country or region hosted a branch of the Society, with a business-like management structure, tasked with logistics in the production and distribution of printed materials. In tacit recognition of the need to drive results, i.e. converts, there was developed an outreach program where each country/region was mapped out so that "Circuit Overseers" might proactively monitor/mentor congregations of individual distributors, designated as "publishers" of the Good News. In a most sophisticated way, groups of circuits were served (read: overseen) by District Overseers, groups of Districts were served by Zone Overseers.

Within individual congregations, men were designated to lead and each congregation had a committee of three, a Congregation Overseer, an Assistant Congregation Overseer and a Service Overseer.

The second aim of the structure of oversight was internal. As with any grouping of humans, standards and procedures needed to be developed and defined. It is a challenging function of human interaction that disputes arise, that measurements must be set in order to adjudicate. This is a more esoteric function than the straightforward decision making about distribution of books, booklets, brochures, leaflets and the like, which decisions were transparent to all.

A subset of this second area of interest was the challenge of conformity to Christian standards of conduct. It is a remarkable distinction of Russell's movement, that respect for Christian standards of conduct was non-negotiable. Many of the iterations of Christendom have fallen on the sword of accommodation of unchristian behaviour and we see the result in the dissipation of so-called Christian societies in our day. Hence, a judicial arrangement was instituted with the intent of spurring respect for those standards. It must be noted that this arrangement, while well intentioned and necessary to establish baseline standards of conduct has become a caricature of itself under the direction of the Governing Body. It is a deeply troubling aspect of the current judicial arrangement that it is used to ferret out such things as individualistic thinking, free association according to personal conscience and, in a truly Orwellian bent, "bad attitude" on the part of adherents. It is apparent that the only measure of "good attitude" is sublimation of one's own conscience to that of the Governing Body, in all things.

At its inception, this judicial arrangement served to accommodate and encourage growth, numerically and spiritually. Motivation was high, trust existed, growth was exponential. Today, this power to intrude into one's life, one's thoughts, has created a climate of condescension and fear - condescension towards any who think outside the narrow confines of official doctrine and fear of ostracism if they should dare to.

Organisationally, a seriously complicating set of factors arose at the end of the tenure of Knorr, when Frederick Franz rose to the presidency of the WTB&TS. One might intuit that the great opposer of truth, the Devil himself, interjected. To be succinct:

1. In the late 1960's, whether due to ego, or ennui, or covetousness, Franz postulated that 1975 was the time for the emergence of the promised New World Order ….

2. At the same time, a cabal of underlings, whether due to ego, or ennui, or covetousness, set out to usurp the power of the Society, and to create a new structure of management….

3. In view of the above two factors, a theory was developed about structure, namely, the theory of the Elder Arrangement….

4. To support all of this, and in view of the organisational inadequacies that have become apparent over time, the mantra of the Governing Body has become -

positivity will bandaid our flaws - be loyal to "the Organization" - we already live in a spiritual paradise - be happy, don't worry.

To explain, the prediction re: 1975 was a life changing marker for many of us. With deliverance into a New World Order imminent, the Elder Arrangement made sense - forget about growth, and cultivate the base. It was further postulated that, with attention thus to quality over quantity, every male could aspire to eldership; the "princes" spoken of in Isaiah were, essentially, elders, and, voila, in theory, we now have a self-governing (theoretically) structure to bridge us the few days, weeks or months until the Kingdom descends from its' seat in heaven when, presumably, the Governing Body and its' supporters will receive their ascension, on the UP escalator to heaven.

Here is the problem: 1975 was wrong, the structure has proven to be ineffective, dynamic leadership has disappeared, and "the Truth" has been subjected to "rule by committee", from top to bottom; this has been a recipe for impotence.

Let me tell you about men, good men, friends of mine, who I love (philia - brotherly love) for their diligence in application of "the Truth" in their lives. Each is a first generation JW, in other words, men who had the courage to come to "the Truth" in a heartfelt way, who progressed to the point of eldership, subsequent to the disappointment of 1975.

Paul Belfontaine - recently I called Paul and we talked like old friends, but on a second call he expressed fear that he was being disloyal in talking to me. Elders, in Paul's day, the Apostle Paul, fearlessly engaged with all manner of heathen, government official, Greek haters of Christianity, even, according to the record of his direction to the Corinthian congregation, encouraging contact with a disfellowshipped one, in the interest of saving a life.

Wally Comeau - during the COVID crisis, I met with Wally. Wally is a loving, sincere man who is so out of touch with reality that he claimed that the CCJW continues to grow apace, citing some fictitious statistic about new congregations in the face of evident cutbacks, amalgamations and sale of Kingdom Halls, even in his own backyard. Wally seems to think that his role as elder is that of cheerleader and, by God, the Governing Body is eager to promote such men.

Jim Healey - a former workmate of mine, and a loving and caring man who has arisen from a disturbed childhood to enjoy the liberation that only surrendering to Christ can bring. Having been schooled about eldership, Jim recently tried to extract from me a kind of confession about my thinking, and my writing, that I am subversive and that the only answer for any of us is repentance, and yet, there is a bigger picture.

Vince Warner - a beneficiary of the 1975 divide, raised by a JW mother and a non-JW father, he leaned into his father up to the point where he accomplished his education. Once secure in his career, he leaned into his mother and "found" the Truth. At a time when our paths crossed, I asked him why he, as an elder, did not take an interest in justice; his answer - "I don't know".

The superstructure which now rests atop the hull constructed by Russell, repaired by Rutherford, tested for seaworthiness by Knorr, sits in a virtual drydock, <u>festooned with lights and banners proclaiming "paradise has arrived"</u>. The WTB&TS has been relegated to handservant of this cabal of men, possibly well intentioned, who, nevertheless, have demonstrated their lack of fidelity.

CHAPTER 14: ALL THINGS TOGETHER IN THE CHRIST

It is a sad truth that Christianity is so splintered. There are many good hearts who, by circumstance, by inheritance, by disparity, are locked into varying schisms of the original worldview of our Messiah. The scriptures tell us that "all things will be brought together"; this is a happy truth!

There was a coming together once before in the annals of so-called Christianity. In a most unchristian manner, national sects united to bloodlet the heathens who occupied Jerusalem, and had the temerity to call it a "crusade'. Jesus said at Gethsemane, "those who live by the sword will die by the sword", thus pointing out the futility of the tribal and nationalistic warring which plagues the history of mankind and of nations referred to as "christian", and, anyway, of what value is an enforced unity? The bringing together, the unity, in line with the loving personality of Jesus Christ, will be through the power of attraction - a uniting of human hearts in peace, love and respect.

Remember that, at its conception, the initiative of CTR was non-denominational. It was a melting pot for the disaffected in every version of Christianity….and what thinking, observant person is not offended by the hypocrisy, the blatant politicisation of mainstream Christendom? However, having become a denomination, a religion, under the direction of the Governing Body, the CCJW is sadly disqualified from playing a uniting role within the Christian world; indeed, the very mention of the name "Jehovah's Witnesses" elicits rancour in many quarters.

Hence, in order to fulfil this role, change, or reversion, is required. Going forward, we must be known, once again, as The New World Society. The timing for such an adjustment is now.

Time has always been a preoccupation of the followers of the true God. Recall that, at the time of the Messiah's appearance on the earthly scene, there was a general expectation that the time was right amongst the Jewish people, and there is a consciousness today amongst Christians of every denomination, that the cacophony, the ugliness, which surrounds us is a signal for change, as promised in Christian writings, and there is scriptural basis for such an expectation.

Now, Russell, Franz, and many Christian prognosticators have been fixated on actual dates in their projections; this has proven to be folly. We might accept that 1914 was significant, that it ushered in the Biblical "time of the end". As an aside, 1914 was arrived at, by Russell, after numerous previous suggested dates, so, if he finally got it right, it was less inspiration than trial and error. Nevertheless, we have clearly been living in an end time for quite some time as evidenced, not by linear measure, but by qualitative measurement of the degradation of the foundations of life - our ecosystem, our social system, our very way of life.

So, we read with interest the phrase "at the full limit of the appointed time" in the letter Paul addressed to the Ephesians; we have arrived at this juncture. Continuing on, we are promised a "[new] administration". And, we know that, beyond Harmageddon, the heavenly administration, the

Kingdom, will hold sway. Those who have led Russell's movement profess kingly rank, and as such, their expectation is for a migration heaven ward, leaving oversight of the earthly arrangement under the Kingdom of Jesus Christ to the "princes" spoken of in Isaiah.

As in any relay race, transition is not accomplished at a single moment in time and space. There is a period of overlap as the new carrier of the baton catches up and then surpasses, and we are grateful that the prior leaders can modestly move on to their heavenly calling. Even if we credit the Governing Body with maintenance of the movement, it is time to install new leadership.

We can expect more than just nuanced change: the spiritual paradise will be supplanted by a literal cleansed earth, the invitation to honest hearted ones will be freed from any need to squabble over doctrine, the issue of Universal Sovereignty will again come to the fore, the Jesus Christ in the manger, the Jesus Christ pictured as a meek lamb delivered to slaughter, will revert to a kingly god of war, as referred to in the Revelation. The scriptures, again, confirm this understanding: when we read of "new scrolls" being opened in the Revelation, a book inspired and written with our time in mind, we conclude that all precepts and principles will be re-thought, under the guidance of the Holy Spirit.

Perhaps the most significant detail when considering just how big a change this will be is the thinking provoked by the word used in roughly half of all Bible translations alternate to "administration" in the book of Ephesians, namely, "dispensation". Again, let us consult

Dictionary.com:

Administration - the <u>management</u> of any office, business, or organisation

Dispensation - the <u>divine ordering</u> of the affairs of the world

It must be said that Russell, Rutherford and Knorr, in consultation with experienced spiritual men, some of whom undoubtedly had solid administrative skills, fashioned an administration that served need within Jehovah's arrangement, and, as is the pattern of His dealings, Jehovah God allowed this leeway, and blessed it, for a time. Therein is the rub, though, left to his own devices, mortal man will, more often than not, go astray.

A dispensation does not allow such latitude. We live in too important a time to rely on the vagaries of imperfect men.

Ephesians, chapter 1 is a preamble of Paul, reflecting on the divine order and the process of selection of those who would reign as kings in the Kingdom of our Lord. Paul, and all spirit anointed ones, have a certainty about their calling. Does it not make sense, does it not harmonise with Paul's assertion, that the "princes" of that Kingdom would also be selected as part of the "divine ordering of the affairs of the world"?

When Paul speaks prophetically of "bringing all things together in the Christ", it implies that the entire Kingdom Arrangement would be God-appointed....... a superlative King, tested and proven Co-Regents numbering 144,000 and earthly Princes who, much like King David in Israel, demonstrate heart quality that qualifies them, in God's view, for this privilege of service.

And what can we say about the bringing of all disparate Christian sects back together?

I will say this, with certitude; my own life experience has taught me that there are people of good heart in <u>every</u> Christian denomination, and this recognition came as a shock to me. I was raised in, immersed in, the culture of the CCJW.

It is a troubling reality that this organisation, to which God's name has been attached, and which, in times past, has clearly been blessed, has mistakenly taken on a "superior air". Twice now, in this missive, I have referred to modesty and humility - Charles Taze, in my view, was modest yet not particularly humble (his dealings with his wife arise here) and Hector Curtis was, in my view, humble yet somewhat immodest. In the CCJW today, the people who are tasked with its' operation are neither humble, nor modest. It is such a shame!

If we are to be the mechanism by which things are "brought together in the Christ", some soul-searching is required.

The operation of the CCJW might be called Orwellian. Meetings, conventions, and special events are now dominated from atop the hierarchy with disproportionate reliance on digital "productions". Local brothers are less teachers than they are emcees to the Governing Body show. No wonder individual enthusiasm and participation is waning!

In fact, the standardisation across presentation via video has diminished the personal ministry which has driven growth in the Christian congregation since the time of the apostles. There is no one-size-fits-all solution. As in the early days, each person privileged with knowledge of the "good news of the Kingdom" must reflect on how to accomplish this bringing together, must reason from and appeal to the heart. Just as Hector Curtis and his comrades in full time service worked independently, and together, to spread their faith. It will affect how you approach your ministry, how you project yourself in your everyday life, how you draw out the good hearts who have thus far held back from commitment to "the Truth".

With godly reliance, with prayerful positivity, each of you will develop a personal ministry.

And, just as in the day when the majority of publishers were heaven-bound, and "10 men hung on to the skirt of a Jew [a spiritual Jew]", so the 8.7 million active associates are hereby assigned the goal of saving 10 others, each one of us. We are hereby freed from "counting time" - henceforth we will count only saved souls - those who recognize the ark of survival in our day!

CHAPTER 15: LEADERSHIP

One of the scriptures, often used to justify the committee approach to decision making, states the principle that "in a multitude of counsellors there is safety". A consideration of the context qualifies this proposition:

Proverbs 24:5,6 reads, variously….

New World Translation - A wise man is powerful, and with knowledge a man increases his power. By skillful direction you will wage war, and through many advisers there is victory.

Complete Jewish Bible - A wise man is strong; yes, a man of knowledge grows in strength. For with clever strategy you wage your war, and victory comes from having many advisors.

Amplified Bible - A wise man is strong and a man of knowledge strengthens his power. For by wise guidance you can wage your war, and in an abundance of wise counsellors there is victory and safety.

Another quotation, from a Watchtower study article, delivers to us how this scripture has been applied - "A body of elders produces a balancing effect as to judgement of matters. While group decisions may seem to take longer, they are more solidly based and, in the end, save time. Truly, "in the multitude of counsellors there is salvation." WT75 8/1 pg 470

Let us dive into this.

Clearly, the counsellors of this Proverb play an advisory

role to support a decision maker, a leader.

In time of war a command structure is critical. A wise commander, a strong commander, relies on the considered advice of his underlings, nevertheless, in the interests of expediency, and to eliminate the chance of mixed messaging, having considered all viewpoints, all advice, a go forward plan of battle is forged by a commander or a captain or a ruler, and must be adhered to. The hoped for result is victory. A committed, well-coordinated army will also minimise risk, by working according to plan, thereby fostering relative safety. A "multitude of counsellors" can inform a decision; the decision maker is responsible for the outcome. In practice, the "balancing effect" of a multitude of counsellors with no clear leader, no decision maker, is consensus or compromise or, at worst, impotence. I have it on good authority that the policy of the Governing Body is to require unanimity to move forward on any matter. Unanimity is not a commonly occurring human state. Even the Supreme Court of the United States renders a variety of verdicts, ranging from unanimity to majority/minority opinions. To require unanimity in all decisions is to dumb down to the lowest common denominator, a recipe for timidity and the status quo.

We are in a war, today, as Christians, and our enemy is none other than the great Satan. This war is about to enter its final phase. How important that adjustments be made to restore true leadership in Jehovah's earthly arrangement. The heavenly arrangement for governance of the New World Order, the Kingdom, is clear - one King, Jesus Christ, a cohort of advisers, serving as adjunct kings, and priests, as counsellors. The earthly component of that rulership will be led by "princes", according to Isaiah.

And, remember, the primary implication of a "dispensation" versus an "administration" is divine ordering, as in selection by holy spirit, as we understand the assignment of the role as co-rulers in the heavenly Kingdom. Is it any less important to leave the selection of princes to God?

It has been suggested that the princes spoken of in Isaiah, in his new world prophecy will be selected, exclusively, by implication, from amongst the elders within the hierarchy of the CCJW. Please consider a pattern of dealings on the part of Jehovah God, in times past:

- David was selected and anointed king of Israel from outside the royal line of King Saul - Jonathan, Saul's son, was a lover of God, a modest man who had much in common with David, and yet, David was anointed, and he was the youngest of his brothers - David was selected by God because of his heart quality

- Amos was gifted with the privilege of speaking truth to power, to the Israelite leaders of his day - he delivered a strong message of reproof, just as I do now to the leaders of God's people today - Amos was an agricultural worker, a nipper of figs - he was selected because of his heart quality

- Jeremiah so incensed the leaders in Jerusalem that he was thrown down a well, as I have been these many years, disfellowshipped, slandered, refused entry at meetings, ignored, thus far, in all my approaches - Jeremiah was selected due to his heart quality

- Saul, later the <u>Apostle Paul</u>, was a ranking Pharisee and a persecutor-murderer of early Christians - Jesus Christ himself designated Paul to be his emissary - before his anointing Paul was an intellectually strong, though misguided man - his writings demonstrate fidelity to the core principles of Christianity - his letters of admonishment stirred great resentment amongst early adherents of "the Way" - Paul would no more fit in to the construct known as the Christian Congregation of Jehovah's Witnesses than Paul would have if he acquiesced to the religiosity extant in the early Christian congregation of his day - he was a bulwark against the dominating influence of "formal worshippers" and "superfine apostles"; such ones dominate us today in the CCJW, from the seat of power embodied in the Organization, led by the Governing Body.

As an aside, the current administration, the Governing Body, has divested itself of the responsibility of overseeing the appointment of elders in the CCJW; such a dilution signifies a laxness, a dereliction. It encourages the politicking that manifests as ambitious men peddle influence to a single Circuit Overseer. At least in times past, there was some semblance of fairness and uniformity across the entire spectrum of the Organization and politicking was not quite so brazen.

There have been many notable men who have served the interests of this rulership. Many fine Christian men from the time of Russell to this day have demonstrated commitment, integrity and appreciation; it is from such men that the King, Jesus Christ, will select his princes. These men are the ones who will lead us into a cleansed earth.

Once established on earth, the Kingdom will surely assimilate men of times past, strong men, men of good heart, into this coterie of royalty, as they are resurrected.

CHAPTER 16: THE DYNAMIC OF THE BROTHERHOOD

There has never been a time during the history of Christianity when a state of war has not existed. This war is waged on a personal basis each and every day by those who take up a life fashioned after Christ. As Peter warned, "Be watchful! Your adversary, the Devil, walks about like a roaring lion, seeking to devour someone."

In the wild, any potential prey of any big cat finds safety, relatively speaking, by staying close to the herd. The "great cloud of witnesses" constitutes a herd, a brotherhood of mutual care, support and protection. If we were not at war, in a wider sense, for survival of the human race, this brotherhood would be all that we need.

I refer you to the article, "The Pattern for Brotherhood", g81 10/8 pp. 8-11, and the subheading "Who Controls the Brotherhood?", as follows,

"Since a brotherhood ...is a "family, there must be a "father" able to...win the loving respect of his "children"
     As the Bible points out: "It does not belong to man…. to direct his own step".

"Hence the "Father" of a true brotherhood must be a heavenly one - Almighty God".

"To come to know and really love, and be loved by, both Father and Son is the way to become a "brother " or "sister ", and is also the way to everlasting life".

The article rightly points out that any brotherhood based

on allegiance to any human, whether pope, king or religious leader, has always failed, and will always fail. We, therefore, need to self-examine and divest ourselves of loyalty to any man, or group of men, including the self-appointed, self-exalting Governing Body.

Respect between brothers is key to the value of the brotherhood; we all answer to the same God. He has endowed each of us with the faculty of conscience and the ability to learn, to come to know his ways. This effort is non-hierarchical. It is a tradition of all religions to look to a central authority for direction, and guidance in these matters. It is a mark of true Christianity that each individual assumes this task, and that, while this brotherhood is at unity of purpose, uniformity is not the goal! The imposition of "matters of conscience" from any central authority works against the exercise of Christian freedom; the Governing Body revels in the making of rules, leaving local elders to apply them. Now elders are provided with long lists of procedure, in reaction to the sad mishandling of CSA (Child Sexual Assault) in the past.

Nonetheless, we can learn from each other. This is why, in the book of Hebrews, Paul asked that there not be, "the forsaking the assembling of ourselves together.... but exhorting, and so much the more as ye see the day coming nigh", Young's Literal Translation, and we are thankful to the "faithful and discreet slave" for provision of much thought provoking material, as we each, individually, shape our consciences, and our lives, around application of principle......and no two lives, or consciences, are exactly the same.

The faithful slave was defined as the amorphous grouping of spirit-anointed alive at any given time in the time of the end; those whose thoughts and writings were received by the Watchtower Society and summarised, refined and delivered via published works and through public address at the various assemblies, conventions and media utilised over time.

In fact, this is the very meaning conveyed in use of the term "society", as in, New World Society; this was the strength of the arrangement under Russell. In the early days of Russellite activity, discussion, dissection and debate led to an understanding of the emerging truths that characterised the movement. This group effort, through diversity of participation, fostered an open and dynamic exchange and explains the early growth of the movement.....a refreshing departure from the top-down dictates of mainstream Christendom, and, sadly, the Governing Body of the CCJW-WTB&TS.

Now, back to the point of departure for the sequence of thought which started this chapter: it is a characterization of human endeavour that hierarchies form, often by design, sometimes by osmosis. It is our contention that no such hierarchy, no caste system, no divide between rich & poor, freeman & slave, formed in the first century congregation; the writings of Paul, James and others were a bulwark against this tendency. James specifically singled out the danger of favouritism based on wealth or social standing. Paul called out formal worshippers and superfine apostles, who emerged in the early congregation. Indeed, Jesus, in a kind of reverse approbation, praised the widow who donated two small coins of little value out of her need, in juxtaposition to the braggarts who made a showy display of their much more significant donations, doing so in public view, out of their abundance.

So, what part did the leadership structure of the legal entity, the WTB&TS, play in the development of the movement? Russell's intention was to maintain the WTB&TS as a repository of true christian teaching, and as a facilitator in the dissemination of the truths thus developed.

Now, there are many critics extant who point out that each of Russell, Rutherford, Knorr and Franz, the four first Presidents of the WTB&TS, were idiosyncratic in their respective ways and, certainly, one need not search too hard to find their flaws. They were, after all, imperfect! Nevertheless, we marvel at the trajectory of the movement, at least until the end of the 20th century, and we, each of us, hear the "ring of truth" in the core teachings which emerged, under guidance of holy spirit, and the true measure of the attractive power of these truths has been the growth of the movement over its' history, until about the year 2000. These powerful and motivating teachings still attract honest hearted ones to the CCJW.

Sadly, the attracting power of said truths, today, is nullified by the tyranny of order which has been imposed on the movement by the cabal of men who comprise the Governing Body. In seizing control, in presuming that they are authorised to lead as a collective, in creating a hierarchical structure where all adherents must abjectly submit to their flawed, reactive, manipulations, this tyranny is clearly manifest. There is no more powerful proof than the legal and social resistance currently at play in the judicial authorities of governments around the world, in Australia, New Zealand, Norway, the USA and elsewhere.

Why else are would-be contributors of new thought, of energising spirit, of ideas stimulated by heartfelt appreciation and their exercise of free moral agency be forced to submit to a hierarchy that stopped innovating by the end of the 20th century? The excessive use of videography cannot be called innovative - quality of life has been diminished by the digital world in which we live, the meta-verse.

Why would subjecting to a small committee of men, focused on rule making and endless revision of doctrine, become stuck, bogged down, once they took over? I mean, I recently attended a public talk in Sussex, NB, delivered from an outline that was assigned to me 40 years ago, when I served as an elder. Stagnation, dismissal of all thinking except that of 9 or 10 or 20 men who comprise the Governing Body, all of whom, by nature, depend on a 50-year-old status quo to establish their value. This is a self-destructive tyranny which is overseeing the death of a movement once blessed by Jehovah God.

And what shall we say of the caste system which now exists at the congregational level…. the tyranny here is a higher caste of elders in each congregation whose appointment, whose continued place of privilege, is entirely dependent on one thing only, their loyalty to men! These men are elevated above other congregation members. They are said to have special insight into the lives of others. They make life changing decisions about congregation members and form judgments which are hidden away in a dark and shadowy vault of gossip known only to them.

This prying and posturing is facilitated by a Service Desk at each branch, that maintains meticulous record of misdeeds of individual congregation members. It is an abomination which induces fear and distrust....and which clearly did not help to prevent or stop the mishandling of child sexual abuse, amongst other things.

Years ago, around 2008, while disfellowshipped I stopped by the Canada Branch of the WTB&TS. I asked to meet with a member of the Service Desk and spent the better part of an hour in discussion with two young Elders whose responsibility it was to work the desk. It had become clear to me that local elders who I had dealings with were operating under the direction of such men as these. It is the policy of the Service Desk that, once a decision is rendered in regard to any given Jehovah' Witness that had been brought to their attention over appearance before a Judicial Committee in any local congregation, such decision could <u>NEVER, EVER be re-examined or revised</u>.

It is galling to me that professional judges and jurists are often subject to appeals, to re-examinations of their decisions, and are found, notwithstanding years of legal training, to have made errors in judgement or application of law. And yet, the judges of the CCJW, who do not claim any divine inspiration, who are subject to making mistakes in the conduct of even their own lives and who are not held to account in the life-changing judgments they impose are subject to no answerability in practise. The earliest followers of Jesus Christ, his disciples, were called "unlettered and ordinary" by his critics, as are virtually all Elders of the CCJW. The earliest elders and apostles did not exercise the overbearing authority which is evident in the CCJW today.

The hierarchy which dictates the community of Jehovah's Witnesses has amply demonstrated the inadequacy of the current arrangement. In regard to CSA, to DISFELLOWSHIPPING & SHUNNING & ARCHAIC ADHERENCE TO THE LAW OF MOSES; therefore, as to administration of the congregation, these men, as a Governing Body, must answer....and according to Matthew 24:45-48, they will.

They have driven away, either by disfellowshipping, disassociation or disparagement, all of the resources, the energies, the passion, the creative thinking ability that once characterised this marvellous movement.

" The biggest concern for any organization should be when their most passionate people become quiet.

We wish to stipulate that the presence of elders, ministerial servants and a "large army" of long serving sisters within the brotherhood constitute a resource. That the return of an advisory, rather than an authoritarian, function for these, for elders in particular, constitutes a valuable resource of knowledge and experience. As in the early days, leadership will be empowered congregation by congregation, circuit by circuit, with an emphasis on coordination in accomplishing the re-invigorated proclamation of Jehovah's day.

CHAPTER 17: THE ARK OF SURVIVAL

So, from a practical point of view, what must be done to restore the modern day "ark of survival"?

First of all, the ark will be re-christened as the New World Society. The designation, CCJW, or Jehovah Witnesses has been counter-productive, for all the boost its adoption provided. The misdeeds of the Governing Body, and the result of policy mistakes from that small coterie of men, all of whom lack vision, foresight and innovation in their thinking, have served to defame the name of Jehovah God.

Next, we harken back to another initiative of Rutherford, which preceded adoption of the new name. During a nine-day convention at Cedar Point, OH held September 1922, the rousing invitation was pronounced, directing adherents, IBS members, to "advertise, advertise, advertise…." the King and his Kingdom. This time, the lead will be taken by the Princes of the Kingdom Arrangement, those anointed by holy spirit to fulfil their earthly role as part of the Kingdom Arrangement. We hereby restate that directive to each of you and we will undertake to lead those efforts.

The ark of Noah's day was readily visible to the world community of that time. As a result of Noah's witnessing outreach, there were certainly questions raised as to the purpose of this never before seen structure; the ark of survival in our day must become similarly visible to all mankind. Thus a major media blitz is needed to stimulate interest, as a beacon for mankind. An outreach through the media, digital and otherwise, rather than singular reliance on attracting an audience to JW.org. This symbiotic relationship between media presence and personal witnessing will draw right-hearted ones to join us in a groundswell not seen since the days when Russell reached his audience through the media of his day.

Think of a couple of Biblical events that illustrate a change in the terms of engagement with our audience. This will be a departure from the arbitrary requirements for months of study and meeting attendance, followed by an oral examination by elders:

The enjoining of a "vast mixed crowd" to the Israelite exodus from Egypt - we raise the question, what prompted these to leave when the Israelites departed Egypt? The evidence points to their recognition of the power of the Israelite God, as evidenced through the ten plagues inflicted on the Egyptians. Was there any requirement imposed upon those right-hearted ones.... circumcision, according to Jewish law? .... completion of a course of study? The urgency of the moment precluded any such precondition."

The requirement that the Israelites turn toward a copper replica of a serpent, on a staff, to escape their dire situation - the scriptures themselves tell us, "as Moses lifted up the serpent in the wilderness, so must the Son of man be lifted up, that whoever believes in him may have eternal life".

It also seems appropriate that the prickly path to reinstatement will be softened, or even abolished. It is surely in-line with the teachings of Christ, as illustrated in the parable of the prodigal son, that re-integration should be much more welcoming and less onerous.

There will be time for education beyond Harmageddon; the critical priority is to recognize the source and the arrangement for survival.

The authority, within Jehovah's arrangement, for deliverance is the Kingdom of which Jesus Christ is King. There have been a number of off-putting reactions to the precedence that the CCJW has put on recognition of Jehovah as our source of life, and as the ultimate source of our deliverance from the imperfect human condition and the system it has spawned. In rebranding the movement started by Russell as the New World Society, we are served with the opportunity to direct attention to the jurisdiction to which Jehovah has delegated authority.

This is significant: There is opportunity to dispel the opinion, formed by many, that the message of the CCJW devalues Christ Jesus; and we must say that, like the ancient Jews, who expressed concern about the overuse of the Divine Name, we need to be circumspect in this regard, also, going forward.

There has been a preoccupation with real estate under the governance of the last 50 years. Recently a major overhaul of the Canada Branch of the WTB&TS was announced, along with a state-of-the-art video production facility at Ramapo, NY. This surely denotes a relegation of our lifesaving outreach in favour of projects of questionable value, considering our place at the full limit of the appointed time.

We cannot predict all of the initiatives that will be undertaken. As in the early Christian congregation, when controversial matters required adjudication and when priorities were reset by a gathering of apostles, elders and others at Jerusalem, wise and experienced counsellors will be assembled to determine a "go forward plan".

CHAPTER 18: A TRADITION OF SPEAKING OUT

Early Christians, as recorded in the Holy Scriptures, declared far & wide the Christian message, with fervour and without fear. For a time, they were horribly persecuted. They carried on undeterred, willing to face death, anchored by faith.

Throughout history, in response to religious abuses by the dominant hierarchies of religion in Rome, in Germany, in England, and elsewhere, those who strove to apply Christianity according to Biblical understanding and conscience, spoke out with a conviction, inspired by their faith in a heavenly reward for their conscientious application of Christian teachings. Many experienced gruesome torture and death from the dominant religious hierarchies of their time and place. Following the lead of Russell himself, his earliest followers demonstrated immense courage, and a measure of irreverence….in confronting the evident hypocrisy of the Christianity of the four estates…. where such religious practices contributed to the subjugation, and relative poverty, of the working classes, in the name of social order. RELIGION IS A RACKET AND A SNARE! was the mantra of the early followers of Russell.

It must be acknowledged that a false sense of entitlement, which muddied the perception of this movement, especially in retrospect, as manifest in a penchant for making predictions dates especially, 1870, 1890, 1914, 1925…and in conceptual statements, too, such as, Millions Now Living Will Never Die. Forgive me if I disappoint you here these were mistakes, ego-driven, from men who took their responsibilities seriously they were not hucksters, as some suggest, they were sincere; and the contemporaneous evidence is that they were taken seriously. The movement succeeded despite such prevarication.

Having gained acceleration from inception, from Russells charisma, having survived what should have been fatal disappointment, from Rutherford's hubris, having seized the moment as a new world order emerged after the Second World War, led by Knorr......the CCJW entered a phase of incremental growth and, again, found a voice on the world scene.... this time, a critical voice in establishing human rights.

Hayden Covington was a legal presence in the USA aligned with the CCJW. He fought successfully to establish religious freedom in the USA and was foremost in legally establishing the now recognized position of conscientious objection as a defence against conscription.

Just as importantly, here in Canada, a figure arose in the person of W. Glen How. How took on the task of freeing Canadian jurisprudence from a tradition of bigotry associated with the dominance of the Catholic Church in the Province of Quebec. Under the Premiership of Maurice Duplessis, a period known as the Great Darkness enveloped the province, unimpeded within Canadian law; it was a time of undue influence by the wealthy industrialists who exploited natural resources in the province, and used the working class in an exploitative way. Concurrent to this, Duplessis acted as the emissary of the Catholic Church in persecuting the JW's, known in French as "Les Témoins".

Glen How is revered as a Canadian legal legend, as he used the courts to establish important freedoms, which now reside in the Canadian Bill of Human rights, and are enshrined in the Canadian Constitution - freedom of association, freedom of assembly, freedom of speech.

All of this makes it exceedingly ironic that the still existing legal entity, W. Glen How & Associates, the flagship of this esteemed Canadian legal icon, is used to deny rightful examination of the suppression of basic human rights within the current iteration of Russells movement - the Christian Congregation of Jehovah's Witnesses. I speak here of suppression of rights under the guise of religious control - not at all protection of the flock...... protection of the religious entity and its hierarchy.

More than this, there exists a quasi-legal mechanism, within the CCJW, for imposition of rules of conduct that contravene the very human rights that Glen How championed. This mechanism is called the Judicial Arrangement, whereby elders sit in judgement of adherents to the faith. At its inception, it concerned itself with deviation from Christian standards of conduct. Today, there is little due process, no right of appeal and very little Christian mercy its application. It induces fear that compels adherents into submission to the religious hierarchy; it is a direct contravention of the example of Christ, and of the writings of Paul.

I must digress here with an anecdote that might inform the reader of the hypocrisy at play here:

Glen How was gifted with high intellect and was a well-educated man (a rarity in the CCJW). I have it on the best authority, the testimony of a long time JW, Blair Weller of Burlington, Ontario, Canada, that, subsequent to his outstanding successes in Canadian Courts, he was hounded by elders in his local congregation (of JWs) for being, somehow, arrogant, or condescending, towards those appointed as elders (forgive me, I know many fine, upright elders, who serve rather than govern). In his later years, at least in part due to the inhospitable environment within his local congregation, Glen How was removed to live out his days at the Canada Branch of the WTB&TS.

Forgive me further as I recount a related anecdote:

In Maoist China, after the fall, after the ascension of communism, there was a prince of royal blood, a former prince, who submitted to communism, as in, life in a commune; he was regarded with a certain disdain, which disdain was extant in the victimhood of the oppressed masses and percolated for many centuries. He stood no chance, really; he was brought before a judicial committee of the commune for the high crime of bad attitude (a familiar charge against all non-conforming JW's); as one avenue of proof, he was charged with pissing into the centre of the bowl, at night, an act of obvious non-conformism, and was hanged.

In each case, feeble-mindedness is evident, and dangerous.

In the devaluation of leadership, in the ascension of every male who might genuflect to the rule of the 9 or so wise men, the 9 headed Pope of the CCJW, in the dilution of leadership, in the impotence of this sad body, Glen How now rolls over in his grave as his legal firm defends the domination of the Governing Body and its' subservient Elder Bodies!

Every single elder I have met (OK there used to be a few who showed compassion) proves his bona fides by damning supplicants to a hell that surpasses the Baptist hell, the Catholic hell…..we will deprive you of all love, family love, brotherly love, self-love…..welcome to hell on earth.

CHAPTER 19: THE MEANING OF JUSTICE

The great overriding systems that define human knowledge are referred to as "disciplines", as in disciplined thinking; medicine, the law, academia, science, all provide a means of understanding life; constructing systems within which humans can live, work and play, and make progress, is a just use of such knowledge. Progress requires cooperation, at least, or coordination from some recognised authority.

The need for justice arises from the challenge of working together; it is a truism that, in pursuing progress, in setting goals, in allocating resources, not least of which is the human resource, problems arise. Human progress is most often a function of that awful and necessary word, ORGANISATION.

The Bible helps us to understand that we are free moral agents and, as such, we are endowed with the faculty of conscience. No two consciences are the same; our innate sense of right and wrong is shaped and refined by our experiences, by our education and by our diligence in growing our "inner person".

Justice is the remedy for the clashes of conscience that are inevitable within the human experience.

On a societal level, good governance requires the proper exercise of authority. At its most elemental level, the exercise of authority, including the justice systems of government, can be a forceful tool, an instrument often wielded bluntly, to restrain, to punish and to maintain order.

Within the congregation of true Christians justice is, or should be, a much finer exercise. In fact, justice in the Christian sense does not require any authority whatsoever. When Christian consciences clash, when they lead to some transgression against the conscience of another, mutual respect for Christ would be enough to bring about equilibrium between brothers. Equilibrium, in this sense, is a descriptor of justice.

The scriptures speak of God's laws (more correctly, God's principles) being written in the heart, or the conscience. As such, they guide us in the outworking of our lives.

The scriptures further speak of the perfect mechanism for achieving justice within the Christian community, namely, Matthew 18:15-17.

Now, clearly, the outward manifestations of the justice systems of this world are absent entirely from the procedure the Christ himself laid out - no courtrooms, no lawyers, no bailiff, no police required.

This does not mean that justice comes easily for Christians; it requires work. It requires a well honed set of personal values, a sense of what issues are worth fighting for and a high tolerance for points of view other than our own.

So, it is just as true within the Christian framework as it is in the legal systems of government that the following underlying principle applies:

"everyone gets exactly what they are willing to

settle for"

Societal justice is extremely expensive. It is often and mostly fuelled by money and, once in a while justice is served; but the legal system is really about laws - their application, their manipulation, their obfuscation. I have never met a lawyer who represented my interest better than I…not that lawyers are irrelevant, by any means…. they are much like doctors: advisors on our journey, with in-depth knowledge of how to handle a crisis, how to navigate "the system(s)" as referred to above.

For Christians, members of the New World Society, justice can only exist as our own personal undertaking. Justice is personal…. and only we (you) know our (your) own trauma, the injustices to which you have been subjected.

It must be noted here, however, that the very mechanism described by Jesus offers a way to escalate a matter, when challenges in resolving differences arise. Can we say, though, that asking a trusted friend, a fellow Christian, to get involved in a discussion/dispute between two others is a case of invoking authority? Not at all.

The CCJW is not the only religious entity to have set out to create a judicial "authority" within the framework of their respective religions. The excesses of the Catholic Court of Star Chamber and, indeed, the Crusades themselves demonstrate the danger of setting up religious judicial authority. And the point must be made here that the use of force to impose Christianity is not reflective of Christ's teaching; what, though, about a judicial authority within the Christian congregation?

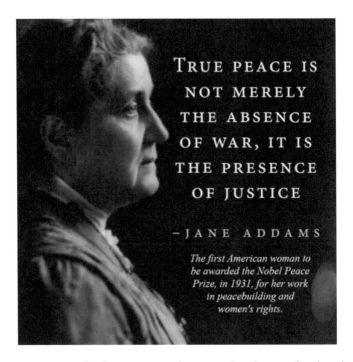

TRUE PEACE IS
NOT MERELY
THE ABSENCE
OF WAR, IT IS
THE PRESENCE
OF JUSTICE

–JANE ADDAMS

The first American woman to be awarded the Nobel Peace Prize, in 1931, for her work in peacebuilding and women's rights.

As a practical matter, the confession of sin is recommended in Christian writings; the exhortation is to "confess your sins to one another". Also, in the early Christian congregation it is clear from comments in the early Christian letters that a public stand was to be taken in regard to Christian standards of conduct, notwithstanding respect for the faculty of conscience. The confessional, properly exercised, is a tool of recovery, of honest disclosure, of acceptance and healing.

It is a sad reality that preoccupation with sin diminishes the healing power of true Christian teaching. CT Russell, remember, liberated many from the fear of eternal torment in hellfire, thus painting the God, Jehovah, as a loving father. More than this, the ransom sacrifice of Jesus Christ provided a basis for forgiveness. These facts can get lost when the arrangement for helping an erring one becomes a mechanism for punishment.

It must also be said that the scriptures tell us, of Jehovah, that it is his preference to look away from our sin.

Considering all of the above, and assuming that, at the inception of a judicial arrangement by Jehovah's Witnesses was a formalisation of the confessional process implemented with good intent, we must say that in its' current form it is ugly, it is overreaching, it is a source of fear and manipulation and it diminishes "the Truth".

Nowhere is this more apparent than in the involvement of the Service Department at Branch facilities of Jehovah's Witnesses. Here, meticulous records are kept of the confession, the sins, the stumblings of adherents to the faith. Here, malicious gossip is practised as Elders and Elder Bodies are "filled in" on lurid details of a person's past.

Here, also, records relating to child sexual abuse have been buried; and, notwithstanding Christ's express instructions that his followers must not judge others, that is exactly what is practised here. It is appalling.

At the congregational level, judicial committees make judgements also; and far beyond the scope of legitimate concern over matters of conduct, there is a preoccupation with "attitude", as if one's attitude might call for discipline.

So what can we say about the caricature of justice embodied by the judicial arrangement of the CCJW, as carried out by authoritarian elders? It is as if congregation members will not do their best to grow as Christians out of heart appreciation. This arrangement is <u>PERVASIVELY JUDGMENTAL, YET LACKING IN DISCERNMENT AND EMPATHY!</u>

CHAPTER 20: AN APPEAL TO STEPHEN LETT

5520 Route 114

Hopewell Hill NB

E4H 3N4 CANADA

April 26, 2023

Mr. Stephen Lett

1 Kings Drive

Tuxedo Park NY 10987 USA

Dear Stephen,

I attach an exchange of letters between Ms. K. McVicar of C.A.Haché Law and Mr. D. Gnam of W. Glen How Associates. I also attach my letter of 23-02-23 to Gnam, written in haste, from the heart.

Ms. McVicar was engaged by me to raise fair questions about adherence to policy and procedure within the Christian Congregation of Jehovah's Witnesses. Mr. Gnam's letter, written on behalf of the elders to whom Ms. McVicar directed her letter, falsely labelled me a "stalker" and impugns my motive in sponsoring Ms. McVicar's letter and, rather than provide any answer, Mr. Gnam dissembles and threatens.

For the record, no Body of Elders has ever expressed to me substantively why I am not reinstated or why I cannot attend meetings; they feel no responsibility to provide any answer. No elder (including successive Circuit JWlett/23-04-26

Page 2

Overseers) has ever engaged me in discussion about the thoughts I have expressed in my many letters. Your own Governing Body has received many letters from me. Why do these letters remain unaddressed?

From Jehovah's point of view (I Kings 18:21), you cannot have it both ways - you cannot claim that the CCJW emulates the first century congregation and, at the same time, impose Catholic-like authority from your pinnacle.

In regard to all of this, I draw your attention to the WT83 9/1 study article "Select Capable, God-Fearing Men". In making the case for the judicial arrangement in the Christian Congregation, this article draws comparisons to the arrangement implemented by Moses in Israel. As with Moses under this arrangement, I take the liberty of escalating my concerns on this "difficult case" to you and to the Governing Body.

Please consider WT83 9/1 par. 18 in the above referenced article, where it is said that "Ambitious men rose up from among the very elders in the congregations. With subverted motives they began to view their office of overseer as a position of power and prestige". Even in the first century, there developed a superstructure of men who wielded power for selfish motive - such ones as these have decided that I cannot even attend meetings. Mr. Gnam says as much when he calls the elders "part-time volunteer ministers", dismissing any role they might play in such a decision.

The "organisation" which was set up to support the great ingathering work prophesied for our time, is populated, at least in part, by men who "view their office of overseer as a position of power and prestige". The early Christian congregation was corrupted in this way; when citing the apostasy which overtook the congregation, "one Catholic historian wrote: "This brought a very great danger…..raising to the most influential sees political men" - WT83 9/1 par.18.

JWlett/23-04-26

Page 3

In view of this threat to the proper exercise of Christianity, I raise alarm to you and to your Body.

There are serious complications arising from this set of circumstances; I do not need to bring to your attention those matters regarding the operation of the CCJW which are public knowledge and that reflect poorly on the name of our God; I am privy to matters involving the internal workings of the "organisation" that are of grave concern and which require immediate attention, in the interests of saving life…. not just the 8 million or so under your care, but at least tenfold more.

As a way of framing this matter, attached is a pertinent sequence of thought; it is an excerpt from the book - Delivering A New World Order - written for the primary audience of the Governing Body of the Christian Congregation of Jehovah's Witnesses. Brother Lett, I am neither subversive nor has Jehovah God abandoned me. My questions and my thoughts are submitted in good faith. I ask that you acknowledge my letter.

Thank you for your consideration.

Best regards,

Mark Warburton

markw@telusmail.net

Attach. 7 pages

EDITOR'S NOTE:

1. The letters referred to in the opening paragraph appear within the Appendix.

2. The chapter referred to in the last paragraph of, and included with this letter, was Chapter 10: What's In A Name, Anyway?, taken from this book.

CHAPTER 21: AN APPEAL TO DAVID SPLANE

5520 Route 114

Hopewell Hill NB

E4H 3N4 CANADA

June 17, 2023

Mr. David Splane 1 Kings Drive

Tuxedo Park NY 10987 USA

Dear David,

I recently read a summary of your comments, delivered from the public platform at a convention in California. I salute you for your forthrightness and for your humour.

The two notable quotes were in regard to coffee breaks (funny, real, thank you) and certain mistakes that were made in regard to 1975, about which I wish to make a comment.

It has been a long time coming; an admission, in any public forum, that the 1975 prediction happened; the issue has been skirted for 50 years. It is curious that, now, you should be willing to acknowledge that which we all have known. There is no point in assigning blame here and now, although we all know that

JWsplane/23-06-17

Page 2

the genesis of this prediction came from Fred Franz. It was embraced by more than a few, though, in Watchtower leadership.

I must tell you that a simple admission, however, does not begin to describe its' effect!

From an organisational point of view, two things happened:

1. The heretofore dynamic organisation turned inwards

2. The theory of oversight known as the Elder Arrangement, pinnacled by the supreme Elder Body, the Governing Body, was instituted.

When I say, "turned inward", I mean that, with the end so near, emphasis was placed on the goal of having each male congregation member aspire to eldership. In times prior, a Service Committee in each congregation was tasked, primarily, with the preaching work, the attraction of new publishers and, of course, respect for the high standards of the movement. Now, had the "end" come in 1975, or soon after, this strategy made sense; and we know that, 50 years on, the end has not happened! and we are left with a declining (quantitatively & qualitatively) congregation.

Must I point out that this arrangement has not proven to be dynamic, at all. Each congregation member is now honour bound to tow a line which requires that elders and elder bodies be put on a pedestal; must be shown loyalty, as a demonstration of faith. This is never what "the Truth" was about.

As to the Governing Body, I pose to you this question:

When has Jehovah God ever commissioned "leadership by committee"?

The Bible answers this question. Time and time again, Jehovah has raised up individual men with just the right qualities and experience to advance His

JWsplane/23-06-17

Page 3

purpose and to lead His people.

Some years ago, I provided to the then President of the Watchtower Bible & Tract Society, Robert Ciranko, and to two of your lawyers here in Canada, David Gnam and Jayden MacEwan, legal documents filed in The Court of The Grand Theocrat (TCGT); I enclose copies of these documents.

TCGT, of course, is not a recognized Court in this system of things. I remind you, however, that at Matthew 24:48-51 it is foretold that there will be an examination of the "fruits" of "the Faithful & Discreet Slave".

In a spirit of forthrightness, I ask that you speak with your fellow Governing Body members about making a defence of your record. Please carry on with the honesty which you displayed at the California convention.

Thank you for your consideration.

Best regards,

Mark Warburton

markw@telusmail.net

EDITOR'S NOTE: The legal documents referred to in this letter follow in Chapter 23

CHAPTER 22: A CALL FOR ACCOUNTABILITY

Let us dispel any doubt - THIS BOOK IS A MANIFESTO FOR CHANGE!

Isaiah, when speaking of the responsibility of a watchman helps us to understand that, apart from a responsibility to act, to speak out, when carrying out a life-saving assignment, there is attendant answerability for a failure to act. This reality is evident as a requirement of justice and can be illustrated by the conduct of security officers in recent school shootings in the USA…..at Columbine the Safety Officer failed to fulfil his mandate altogether by hiding away, at Uvalde hesitation in exercising protective responsibility resulted in unnecessary loss of life and the ultimate dismissal of the supervisor in charge of the operation.

As sketched out in Chapters 20 & 21, there has been an unconscionable abdication by senior members of the Governing Body. These men have long experience serving as Christian elders; how can warnings such these be ignored? Do they not possess any faculty of conscience? Were they out-voted by their peers?

It is a deep flaw of the Elder Arrangement which characterises most, if not all Elder Bodies, including the Governing Body. This flaw is laid out as official policy of the CCJW, under the direction of the Governing Body, in the April 2017 WT Study article entitled "Do You Share Jehovah's Sense Of Justice". In this article it is made clear that elders, as a group, have the right, after consideration of any given matter, to agree on a position, even take action, with no transparency, with no responsibility to explain positions taken. This is a recipe for unprincipled conduct....and I have experienced it firsthand!

More than this, there is no emphasis, whatsoever, on working for justice in dealing with matters involving "sheep" under their watch. For example:

• Matt 18:15-17 prescribes the solution to interpersonal dysfunction; there is no call for a "judicial body" to resolve such problems; in the CCJW elders have been led to believe that they, only, can authorise application of this procedure when, as followers of Christ, they are obligated to accommodate it, whenever asked

• I have heard, often, that elders's primary concern is preservation of the "peace of the congregation"; this is most often cited when contentious personal conflicts arise; as in, be quiet and let Jehovah (we elders) work it out; such passivity is a recipe for impotence and has made the CCJW deplorably lacking in elemental justice, a reality that has turned many of the younger generation to turn away. This is nowhere more obvious than in the exhortation to "wait on Jehovah", while elders do nothing

• The reason that child sexual abuse has occurred with impunity in the CCJW is the spurious idea that reporting such to secular authorities might bring "reproach on Jehovah's name"; thusly, the CCJW has been like a family that enables deviance by a family member by keeping it secret; BADNESS MUST BE EXPOSED!

• "Maintain positivity" in the face of injustice is an oft

cited idea which, essentially, relieves elders, and Elder Bodies, from dealing justly; this is no less true of the Governing Body than any other Elder Body

Isaiah, when describing the "princes" of the New World Order said that they would rule "for justice itself". It is obvious that for elders, generally, elders such as Stephen Lett, the pursuit of justice is subservient to the smooth operation of the machine known as the "Organisation" and preservation of their own comfortable pew.

Further, in the matter of doctrine we note that our leaders, such as David Splane, are incapable of developing innovative teaching that fairly accommodates current realities. As pointed out in the above letter, not only was 1975 a mistake, 1914 was a mistake. We accept that 1914 was a consequential year but the spiritual gymnastics involved in the various rationalisations delivered over the years, the latest of which is the theory of "overlapping generation" is an insult to the thinking, faithful servant of Jehovah God.

An overbearing emphasis on the sins, stumbles and mistakes of its' members pervades the Organisation; not so much the failings of those who have climbed the hierarchy as much as an unfailing reminder to all adherents of the faith, requiring repentance, without exacting the same standard on themselves, individually or as a collective. Most obviously, the elders who work the Service Desk collect, quantify and memorialise every mistake made by a rank and file member; the collection of personal, private information did nothing to mitigate child sexual abuse, so what is the point? If such information is simply a means to control or expel adherents, of what real value is this exercise?

Remember that the scriptures indicate that Jehovah God chooses to "put our sins far off", as far as from the East to the West.

It is not inappropriate to suggest that a review of the "fruits" of The CCJW, under direction of the Governing Body is coming due; at Matt 24:45-51, it is clear that such an examination is prophesied; and there is a sense amongst all Christians that the time for the return of "the Master" is nigh.

Under the headship of Jesus Christ himself, such an examination, such a hearing must take place, just as it did in Jerusalem in the first century, to make examination of policy and practice at that time.

There are many thousands who once identified as JW's, many of whom still do their best to maintain trust and faith in the Great God, through prayer, love & encouragement from those outside the congregation who minister to their need for acceptance and who nourish their self-worth, and, interestingly, even some from those who still maintain membership as JW's, those who have the courage & conviction to override the formulaic rulings of an intrusive & controlling Governing Body.

In regard to disfellowshipping, reinstatement and the associated practice of shunning, the Governing Body is exactly like Donald Trump in that Trump demonstrates the belief that if you tell a lie often enough, and especially if you can get others to repeat the lie, it is accepted as true; the lie, in this case, is that the practice of disfellowshipping, according to the current rules of implementation, is an expression of Christian love. This lie has been oft repeated, in print and from the public platform.

In this regard, we cite a secular source, George Orwell:

"Oceanic society rests ultimately on the belief that Big Brother is omnipotent and that the Party is infallible. But since in reality He is not omnipotent and the Party is not infallible, there is need for an unwearying, moment-to-moment flexibility in the treatment of facts. The keyword here is BLACKWHITE. Like so many Newspeak words, this word has two mutually contradictory meanings. Applied to an opponent, it means the habit of impudently claiming that black is white, in contradiction of the plain facts. Applied to a Party member, it means a loyal willingness to say black is white when Party discipline demands this. But it also means the ability to BELIEVE that black is white, and more, to KNOW that black is white, and to forget that one has ever believed the contrary."

CHAPTER 23: THE COURT OF THE GRAND THEOCRAT

COURT OF THE GRAND THEOCRAT

NOTICE OF MOTION

Dated this 28th day of October, 2019.

On behalf of,

Warburton, Mark et al, Plaintiff

To,

Watchtower Bible & Tract Society of Pennsylvania,
Defendant

Be advised, that a hearing will take place at a time and place to be determined, on the motion attached. The purpose of the hearing will be to investigate possible Articles of Impeachment against the Governing Body of the Christian Congregation of Jehovah's Witnesses who, on the authority of this Court, will be asked to answer for the deficiencies apparent in the operation of the true Christian Congregation.

In bringing motion, we see a need to establish this counterbalancing judicial authority, as above, within the Theocratic Arrangement, on behalf of the Grand Theocrat, Jesus Christ, at this critical time in human history.

Opportunity for self-examination by the Governing

Body has been afforded over a period of years, in response to correspondence submitted as described in the attached affidavit. Fair judgment cannot now be expected of the Governing Body or close associates of the Governing Body within the Organization, considering the inattention to matters, and the coverup of misconduct by appointees and officials of the WTB&TS to date.

There is a vast reservoir of brothers experienced in life and the application of Christian principle to the challenges presented. Drawing on such to administer the Court of the Grand Theocrat would be a modern day equivalent to the Judicial Body assembled in Jerusalem and formulated for the single purpose of adjudicating similarly important questions of procedure and principle in the first century Christian Congregation.

Truly yours,   ——————————

COURT OF THE GRAND THEOCRAT

MOTION

On behalf of,

> Warburton, Mark et al, Plaintiff

To,

> Watchtower Bible & Tract Society of Pennsylvania,
> Defendant

Be it known, that we petition you, as Defendant, to open up an examination of the conduct of the Governing Body of the Christian Congregation of Jehovah's Witnesses (CCJW), in consideration of Articles of Impeachment. We ask for a full and impartial, a just examination of the argument and evidence presented, leading to a decision directing the further development of the timely and expansive work of the Kingdom Arrangement here on earth.

1.   By Divine Providence, over the course of biblical history, men have been raised up to lead the way in the outworking of His purpose for the earth and mankind; such a man arose in the late period of the 19th century in the person of CT Russell.

2.   CT Russell undertook to develop and disseminate true Christian teaching and set in motion a modern day movement, unique in its'

adherence to Christianity; the legal entity which he established as a bulwark within which Christians could worship is the Watchtower Bible & Tract Society (WTB&TS), now present in its many iterations.

3.   By precedent, the WTB&TS has carried primary responsibility for oversight of the true Christian Congregation in modern times; and just as kingly authority and priestly oversight provided counterbalance in Israel, and just as, in a secular setting, the Constitution of the United States recognizes the need for protection against unfettered exercise of power, the seizure of power by the Governing Body along with concurrent subjugation of the WTB&TS has led to this legal motion.

4.   The scriptures, at Matthew 24:45-52, designate an entity tasked with care of the interests of the Kingdom of Jesus Christ, a "faithful & discreet slave", which entity has come to be associated with the WTB&TS; the text introduces the possibility that this entity might become corrupt, or inept, in caring for these interests; this failure would be manifest in the mistreatment of members of the movement.

5.   The Governing Body has laid claim to the title Faithful & Discreet Slave

6.   The teachings of Jehovah's Witnesses foster good quality of life for adherents,

notwithstanding controversy over such things as the use/mis-use of blood; there have been a number of errant predictions that have thrown into doubt the veracity of the leadership structure; the primary marker for fidelity to Christian teaching is in the operational effects of the structure of oversight - "by their fruits you will know them".

7.   For most of the history of the movement there has been growth. We currently see marginal-to-no growth; this is coincident with the maturation of the oversight strategy known as the "elder arrangement".

8.   The movement is characterised, today, by a requirement for abject subjection to the Elder Arrangement, of which the Governing Body is the pinnacle, initiated in the runup to 1975 as a strategy for autonomous survival into the predicted new system. This Arrangement has become overwhelmingly homogenous and authoritarian. A hierarchy of appointees of the Governing Body, Circuit and Branch Overseers, constitute a mechanism of unvarying administration of "the Organization". The teachings of Jesus Christ are liberating and accommodating of individuality; the structure of the Organization is suffocating.

9.   In the matter of discipline, lines have blurred. Punishment is not the goal of Christian discipline; an unhealthy climate permeates the congregations as elders wield unchecked licence in dealing with judicial matters, as delineated in the

April 2017 WT article - Do You Share Jehovah's Sense of Justice?

10.   The Judicial Arrangement is a key component of the Theocratic Arrangement; it applies to all adherents to "the Way", equally, congregation publisher through to GB member.

11.   The attached affidavit of Mark Warburton details an abdication of responsibility for oversight on the part of Watchtower appointees and members of the Governing Body of the CCJW; it also cites instances of abuse of power, in violation of written guidelines of principle and procedure, by at least two individuals, Elder Mihluk of the Victoria Gardens Congregation and Superintendent Jung of the Canada Branch.

12.   We invite our brothers in leadership to make a "defense of faith" before this Court in these matters; and to explain the dereliction of duty in allowing the matters presented herein to go uninvestigated, unanswered and unremedied within the hierarchy of the Organization.

Sworn before the Grand Theocrat at Moncton, New Brunswick

this 28th day of October, 2019.

_____

COURT OF THE GRAND THEOCRAT

AFFIDAVIT

Of,

Warburton, Mark, Plaintiff

Following is a summary of facts and beliefs arising from my experience as a dedicated, baptized worshipper of Jehovah God. I personally have knowledge of the matters herein and I hereby testify that the following is true, to the best of my knowledge, and that I verily believe these facts and beliefs support the Motion to which it is attached:

1.   I am 66 years old, resident of Riverview, New Brunswick Canada and a citizen of the United Kingdom. I was baptized on May 14, 1967 at Burlington, Ontario. I was appointed as a Ministerial Servant at or about May 1975 at Summerside, Prince Edward Island. I was appointed as an Elder at or about June 1983 at Moncton, New Brunswick.

2.   I was raised by god-fearing parents who inculcated in me a primary allegiance to pursuit of Kingdom interests.

3.   In 1969, having graduated from high school at the tender age of 16, I embarked on the life of a "pioneer". My motive was honourable; any

other life choice, in view of the spirit of the times, the 1975 fixation, would have been inconceivable to me.

4.   My high school teachers of the time, Mr. Wigle and Mr. Lewis, strongly counselled me to invest in the development of my talents and skills by pursuing higher education; they did not, in any way, try to subvert my faith; they offered a rational counterbalance to the dominating influence in my life; my father, too, encouraged me to allow myself time to grow by continuing my education.

5.   Unhinged from the discipline of school; vicariously working on a life trajectory inspired by the leaders of the WTB&TS, I became detached from my own best interests.

6.   Having seized license for independent direction of my own life, empowered by the elevated rhetoric to which I was exposed at meetings and conventions of the CCJW, I fell into marriage, fatherhood and the continuum of life as a Jehovah's Witness, common to many of my generation.

7.   Notwithstanding my own lack of modesty in ignoring the voices of reason in my life, I conformed to the JW way of life; a valid measure rests in the advancement from publisher to ministerial servant to elder; without undue consideration of the confluences and influences in my life, it would be fair to say that I made the best

of things.

8.   At or about March 1990, I made request to resign from the privilege of eldership; this did not infer, in any way, my abandonment of the JW way of life; I re-doubled my efforts to lead my family in the way of "the Truth".

9.   At this point, an apparent enemy of mine, a brother in the congregation, started to raise questions as to my motives, my personhood and my standing as a dedicated servant of God. I yearned for peace, away from the pressures of being an example, to rethink my life. This man, Robert Duncan, has been the devil, the slanderer, in my life.

10.   The further following details of my life relative to the motion under consideration hinge on this slanderer, on the way in which the office of elder, the policies of the Governing Body and the worst manifestations of human nature have combined to destroy my good name, my standing in the congregation and my family - notably not, however, my standing before my God.

11.   The truth about slander, about slanderers, is that they use subterfuge; as in, Satan the Devil hid behind a wonderful creation of God; ventriloquism is a required skill in the surgical application of slander. James 3: 5-7, in referring to slander, states "See how small a fire it takes to set a great forest ablaze! The tongue is also a fire. The

tongue represents a world of unrighteousness among our body members, for it defiles all the body and sets the whole course of life on fire." Robert Duncan set a fire in my life; it has spread through expansion and delivery of that slander by his proxies within the true Christian Congregation.

12.   The antidote for slander is application of Matthew 18: 15-17. Elders in Moncton, Toronto and Welland are derelict in opposing my requests for application of Matthew 18 in this matter.

13.   The truth about elders is that it is virtually unheard of that individual elders will stand on matters of conscience when presented with the weight of authority of the Service Desk, as conveyed by a Circuit Overseer, even if there is a clear violation of principle or policy.

14.   The truth about the members of the Governing Body is that, in matters spiritual, they only look at the horizon; they do not wish to be involved in practical matters of deviation from principle or practise on the part of their appointees.

15.   At the beginning of my ordeal, I knew that Duncan was exerting influence over my family members and my friends in the congregation; now, it is true that I, myself, brought about a change in my relationships by resigning my eldership; at the same time, I tried to reach out, in the moment, to reassure others that I was not abandoning my faith and, also, to try to understand the reactions of

others.

16.   I attach my letter of January 04, 2017, addressed to the Governing Body, as Exhibit "A". This letter details a sequence of dealings within the congregation from the time of my resignation, a period of 15 years. Successive Bodies of Elders and Watchtower personnel, Circuit Overseers and Branch Elders, conducted dealings with me in a consistent pattern which reflected bias against me, which ignored a part they could play in application of Matthew 18 and which demonstrated contempt for written and documented Theocratic Procedure.

17.   Receipt of the letter of 17-01-04 was acknowledged by the Legal Department at Patterson; I was told that the letter had been referred to the Canada Branch; I was told by Warren Shewfelt, that he had no interest or obligation to deal with my letter; this is a dereliction of duty and constitutes insubordination to the Theocratic Arrangement.

18.   Amongst many false charges against me, the most serious and damaging charges authored by Robert Duncan are of sexual interference against my niece, Alana Duncan, and his stepson, Jeff Down; elders of the Christian congregation, Peter Schweller and David Dorman elders of the Royal York and Shediac Congregations, respectively, have countersigned his accusation, with no attempt at corroboration, no application of Matthew 18, with full knowledge of, and the direction of, the

Service Desk.

19.   I attach, as Exhibit "B" my letter dated August 11, 1997, addressed to Robert Duncan, asking him to meet with me to discuss his charges with a view to preserving my marriage to his daughter. My efforts a month before my marriage ended were still focused on a face-to-face discussion, as at Matthew 18.

20.   At this time, I beseeched the elders of the Scarlett Heights Congregation, Colin Cummings and Roy Corbett, to work with me in application of Matthew 18, to engage my slanderer and to preserve my marriage; Jesus Christ recommended that face-to-face discussion, with witnesses, might resolve such a problem. I was told no, as if elders have the exclusive right to decide when Matthew 18: 15-18 applies to a given situation.

21.   At this time, I visited the Canada Branch and met with Rodney Jung on the Service Desk; I was not well received; Jung took offense at the nervous anxiety I displayed; my family was under threat by a slanderer, would soon be destroyed at his hand, and no elder would moderate a discussion between he and I; subsequent to this visit Colin Cummings, my Presiding Overseer, informed me that Rodney Jung did not like me.

22.   About this time, Colin Cummings informed me that Duncan had involved a lawyer, on behalf of my wife. Notwithstanding a spiritual

responsibility to bring the parties together, Cummings told me that I should "move on" from my marriage.

23.　On the day of treachery, a Friday, I was at home, tending to my business; I received a phone call from my younger son, Cedric, asking me to be home later in the day; soon after my wife and son arrived home, she incited a confrontation, pummelling me with her fists; as soon as I reached out to restrain her, she screamed to my son to call 911; the police arrived, and I spent the evening in jail.

24.　Not content with destroying my first marriage, Duncan volunteered to support my second wife in a custody battle in court, 2 years later, and filed affidavits alleging another false charge, of mental defect on my part; elders in my congregation in Welland, Ontario joined in this support, accompanying my wife to court; this support was sanctioned by Jung at the Service Desk.

25.　The truth about the Service Desk at the Canada Branch is that, from afar, judgments are made about specific matters and persons, and that local elders are directed in accord with judgments made at the Service Desk. In hindsight, I realize that, starting with my resignation as an elder at or about March 1990, a fabric has been woven at Georgetown Bethel which has incorporated every stitch of my own mistakes and trials, along with a gathering deprecation authored by local elders who wish to support the manufacture; application of scriptural principle and procedure has been secondary to "building a case" that aligns with the judgment of the Service Desk, in my case a metaphor for the personal judgment of Brother Rodney Jung.

26.   Desperately discouraged at the loss of my family and my good reputation as a Christian, I fell into an intimate relationship with my eventual third wife; this woman offered me comfort and support which was lacking in the congregation; the elders in the Burlington, Aldershot Congregation who considered my confession were unsympathetic.

27.   The truth about disfellowshipping for infidelity, within the CCJW, is that there is little consideration of mitigating factors. Theoretically, one could be a rapist, or a child molestor (predatory crimes) or, as in my case, one could buckle at the knees under the weight of slander and judgmentalism, and, from an elders point of view, judgment is pretty much the same. I was summarily disfellowshipped in October 2002.

28.   My third wife and I took up residence in Nova Scotia, in proximity to my 2-year-old daughter by my second marriage, and, together, re-established a spiritual routine of meeting attendance at the Bedford Congregation at or about November 2002, which routine was maintained

through to May 2005.

29.   After re-location to the vicinity of Moncton, New Brunswick, and after having established a record of regular meeting attendance at the Victoria Gardens Congregation, at or about October 2005, I made application for reinstatement, concurrent to my wife's application.

30.   At the first meeting with a reinstatement committee of the Victoria Gardens Congregation, much ado was made of the fact that, in my letter of plea, I had used the salutation "Dear brothers" - as I recall, this was particularly offensive to only one member of that committee, Elder Nik Mihluk.

31.   The truth about those who stumble in serious sin, from the standpoint of Jehovah God and Jesus Christ, and as summarized by the Apostle Paul at 2 Corinthians 2:7,8, is - "now you should kindly forgive and comfort him, so that he may not be overwhelmed by excessive sadness. I therefore exhort you to confirm your love for him". Brotherly love, it seems apparent, can extend even beyond disfellowshipping, in the eyes of God.

32.   Notwithstanding the churlishness of Mihluk, the committee chairman, Robert Hicks, in the presence of Mihluk and Aubrey Kelly, on January 1, 2007, acknowledged my evident repentance and invited me to pen a letter of plea to the Aldershot Committee with the assurance that I would be recommended for reinstatement.

33. I attach the letter dated February 15, 2016 as Exhibit "C", addressed to Mr. Sean Oostdyk and penned by Rodney Jung of the Canada Branch, in which the statement is made "[the] reinstatement process is consistent and transparent; it is outlined in the book "Organized to do Jehovah's Will"…..". Jung was well aware, when he wrote this letter, that he had intervened, through the Service Desk, to deny my reinstatement in January, 2007 - inconsistent with the Organized Book procedure for reinstatement.

34. The Aldershot committee, in considering the recommendation to reinstate from the Victoria Gardens Committee, as conveyed to me by Ernest Downes, Chairman, was contacted directly by both Nik Mihluk and Rodney Jung. Both of these injected their personal biases against me and countermanded the decision of the Victoria Gardens Committee; my plea was refused. Again, a violation of Theocratic Procedure.

35. In December 2009, I participated in a trial in Family Court in Burton, New Brunswick over custody and access to my daughter Sophie, now aged 10 years. During this trial, her mother stirred up prejudice against Jehovah's Witnesses by misleading the Court, in her testimony, as to the teachings to which Sophie was exposed in attendance with me, at the Shediac Kingdom Hall. The false testimony had effect and resulted in a decision to award custody to my former wife and to

severely restrict my ability to bring Sophie to a meeting at the Kingdom Hall, or even a knowledge of the Truth.

36.   In May of 2010, at a follow-up appearance in Court, I subpoenaed a number of persons from Moncton and Fredericton, including some elders, to testify to correct the lies which had been told about Jehovah's Witnesses. The Service Desk dispatched Jayden MacEwen, of the law firm How & Associates, to raise objection to my subpoenas and to subvert my efforts. My legal case was effectively destroyed.; my rights to educate my daughter in "the Way" were permanently undermined, at the direction of the Service Desk.

37.   Some years later, in January 2016 and until November 2016 , I took up residence in Hamilton, Ontario and took up meeting attendance at the Aldershot Congregation and made application directly to Aldershot, for reinstatement.

38.   The truth about my second attempt at reinstatement is that I did not know what the brothers wanted me to confess. I was disfellowshipped for a single act of adultery, committed in an environment of impossible odds against me, no more, no less. The accumulated lore associated with my name was a fabrication of Robert Duncan, delivered to every elder who would listen, across half a continent, and distilled into a file on the Service Desk, at Bethel. I was regarded with deep suspicion; my plea was again rejected.

39.   I attach the letter dated September 20, 2016 as Exhibit "D", addressed to Ms. Karen Morimoto and penned by Philip Brumley, Counsel to the WTB&TS of Pennsylvania. In this letter, in reply to our good faith request for a hearing from the Governing Body over the prejudicial dealings of the Service Desk, Brumley makes the statement "neither the Governing Body, nor any representative of the Governing Body, will grant him an audience", and, " the Governing Body does not involve itself in these matters….".

40.   At Matthew 24: 45-47, the office of "faithful & discreet slave" is specified as the mechanism for oversight of Kingdom interests; the Governing Body claims to fulfill this role; when Moses fulfilled a similar role, as overseer of Israel and God-appointed leader, Exodus 18: 25,26 states "Moses chose capable men. So they judged the people when cases arose. A difficult case they would bring to Moses…"

41.   I attach my letter dated September 14, 2019, addressed to the Governing Body, as Exhibit "E"; this is my latest request to the Governing Body for attention to this longstanding, seemingly intractable problem.

42.   Throughout my entire ordeal, I have kept the brothers at the Canada Branch and at World Headquarters apprised of these circumstances.

43.   The truth about the activities at Bethel,

in Canada and in the USA, is that the brothers are so fixated on their goals and dreams, of leading us into a new world order, that they have no time or attention available for the challenging matters of deviation from the "healthful pattern of words", as laid out in publications of the Society, that I have described.

44.   The following representatives of the WTB&TS have been apprised of great detail in all these matters, and care not at all to consider the implications:

> Douglas Jones, David Cohen, Nik Sederis, Michael Goodwin, all Circuit Overeers; Ken Little, Warren Shewfelt, successive National Coordinators; David Gnam, Philip Brumley, Society lawyers; David Splane, Anthony Morris lll, Stephen Lett, Samuel Herd, Gerrit Lösch, Guy Pierce, Mark Sanderson, Geoffrey Jackson, all Governing Body members.

45.   I currently reside in Riverview, New Brunswick; my latest application for reinstatement at the Riverview Congregation has been suspended by the Elder Body for the sole reason that I have put my concerns in writing, to the Riverview Body and to Bodies of Elders in surrounding Congregations, where my slanderers attend meetings. I have been disinvited from attendance at meetings, including the Memorial celebration for 2019.

46.   I hereby name my slanderers, those who

have taken up the slander of Robert Duncan:

> David Dorman, Robert Hicks, Nik Mihluk, Robert Deamude, Peter Schweller all elders; Cindy Deamude, Sharon Dorman, Shirley Caissie, Carol Down, Donna Matthews, Debra David, Miriam Cohen all sisters in good standing; Robert Duncan Jr, a brother in good standing; David Cohen, Circuit Overseer; Rodney Jung, Superintendent of Ministers and Evangelists at the Canada Branch.

47.   I am a single example, of many, of those brothers referred to at Matthew 24: 49 as a "fellow slave" who has been "beaten" by acts of omission in oversight by the Governing Body, and by acts of commission by those for whose conduct the Governing Body is answerable, Elders of the CCJW and Officers of the WTB&TS.

Sworn before the Grand Theocrat at Moncton, New Brunswick this 28th day of October, 2019.

Mark Warburton

_____

CHAPTER 24: TOWARDS A NEW WORLD ORDER

In the face of the conditions summarised within this treatise, we read with comfort and optimism the promise recorded in the book of Isaiah:

"Look! A King will reign for righteousness itself;

and as respects princes, they will rule as Princes for justice itself"

The Bible promises change at the end of a system of things, the Old World Order. Princes will arise; new scrolls will be opened; a new leadership, with new direction, will replace a once "faithful & discreet slave"* As in times past, the Great God will appoint any new leader. Oversight by committee has run its course.

*We should say here, that if Jesus suggested a that a once faithful slave might take on an evil character, he said it for good reason; "evil" does not necessarily mean "wicked"; it means that a more appropriate form of leadership, for our time, is required to face the challenges ahead.

And here is a thought provoking allegory about openness to change:

The areas of medicine and law are both precedent driven and precedent bounded; they resist change, as does the practise of religion. If you are satisfied with the results of your practices, your traditions and your doctrines, why change?

Brother Walter Graham attended a Circuit Assembly in

Moncton, New Brunswick in the late 1980's to report on the activity of the Medical Liaison Committee. His insightful discourse contains a lesson about the wisdom in accommodating change when convincing evidence and compelling reasoning are presented.

It had been a standard procedure within the medical community to undertake treatment for bleeding stomach ulcers with liberal use of blood transfusion; the success rate in treatment according to this protocol was in the range of 75%, i.e. 3 out of 4 patients successfully recovered.

Now in any life saving work 3 out of 4 would seem to be an acceptable, even a highly desired, rate of success.

Due to concerns about improper use of blood, as defined by the collective conscience of Jehovah's Witnesses, and in view of the fact that the medical challenge of bleeding stomach ulcers occurs regularly with JW's (no more or less than the general population), an approach was made to willing medical professionals to test out a new approach.

Please note that the brothers on the committee are not doctors, but they asked that a new method be considered. In making their case they used an analogy. They reasoned, if a pipe burst in your house, you would call a plumber; the last thing a plumber would consider would be to turn the taps on, above the leak, to full on; this would add higher flow to the leak when dealing with a breached pipe; ergo, they said, we pose this question - why administer more blood when it is leaking right out into the stomach? The acids in the stomach are not conducive to coagulation of blood, so increasing the flow of blood via transfusion seems counter-intuitive, does it not? they asked. Instead, they suggested, why not try packing the stomach with ice, to shrink any swelling, to thicken the blood, to reduce blood leakage? In an amazing confirmation of this logical sequence of thought, and against all precedent, the results dramatically improved to a 95% recovery rate. More than this, there were fewer complications arising from the wide variety of blood factors and, so, recovery time was shortened, again, dramatically.

Now, what is the point of this story?

The past 50 years have not been wasted; the net effect of this time period has been the galvanisation of a nation of 8.7 million loyal servants of the True God. By instituting change now, by submitting to the clear direction of Jesus Christ, Head of the Christian Congregation, many more souls can be added to the ranks of the New World Society.

Not only does the Bible point to change at this time, such change is in the best interests of regaining momentum lost; it is also in the interests of attracting and engaging a "great crowd that no man was able to number", as prophesied in the Revelation. Eight million is a paltry number compared to the sum total of good hearts yearning for deliverance into the New World Order.

It is time to counter the sense of self-satisfaction, the smugness, that permeates the Christian Congregation of Jehovah's Witnesses amongst those who have not left; it is time to move beyond the habits of the past 50 years; it is time to throw off tradition in favour of a new dynamism.

We anticipate the arrival and identification of the princes to lead our march into the "ark of survival". We anticipate that a slave of Jehovah God, once faithful and discreet, now evil, will <u>modestly submit to a new arrangement</u>. We further anticipate new enlightenment, "new scrolls", that will lead us along a process of renewal.

Let the reader use discernment!

I can't stand your religious meetings.
I'm fed up with your conferences and conventions.
I want nothing to do with your religion projects,
your pretentious slogans and goals.
I'm sick of your fund-raising schemes,
your public relations and image making.
I've had all I can take of your noisy ego-music.
When was the last time you sang to me?
Do you know what I want?
I want Justice—oceans of it.
I want Fairness—rivers of it.
That's what I want.
That's all I want.

Amos 5:21-24
The Message

TO MY READERS:

You may have noted that, although my presentation is forthright, both in identifying flaws in the operation of the true Christian congregation AND in naming names, in various notations and in various ways I have taken pain to lighten my message by recognising that <u>much of the deflection away from the original trajectory of Russell's movement has been inadvertent</u>. I HAVE CONDEMNED NO-ONE.

More than this, I have wished for, and I have prayed for, a certain humility, and a measure of modesty, in those who currently direct the CCJW/WTB&TS. Sadly, this is not in evidence as of this date; whether due to lack of basic reading ability, or a careless disregard for the reputation of the Almighty God or, most likely, an unshakeable arrogance based on their inflated sense of self, these men have missed an opportunity to self-correct.

It is my considered opinion that a blithe blindness exists in the Christian Congregation of Jehovah's Witnesses - just as with the Jews of Jesus' day, the collective Elder Body of the CCJW is blinded by a myopic belief that they are somehow "special"; that they are protected in a bubble of (self-)righteousness; ergo, I claim, on behalf of all lovers of goodness, as follows:

Throughout this book, I have used the inclusive pronoun "we", as in we....

● Must address the imbalances extant within the true Christian brotherhood

● Must act justly, must engender justice, in all our dealings, as suggested by the prophet Joel

● Must reverse the damage which has accrued over the last 50 years, to both the movement of Russell and the reputation of the Great God

● Must re-ignite the spirit of the congregations, which spirit has suffered under the administration of the Governing Body

● Must re-jig the Organisation to serve, rather than rule

- Must root out the nepotism and the sense of entitlement evident within the Organisation today

- **MUST RESURRECT THE NEW WORLD SOCIETY**

And, although I have wanted to work within the current arrangement, have invited a cooperative approach repeatedly, it seems that the opportunity has passed.

THEREFORE, the "we" must be understood to simply mean all those of honest heart, i.e. any and all ex-JW's, every current JW and, indeed, as in Russell's day, every person of good heart, in any denomination, of any creed, race or religion, those will prrove to be members of the new, **NEW WORLD SOCIETY 2024.**

We will, by all means possible, advertise, advertise, advertise the only hope for mankind, namely, the Kingdom of Jesus Christ. We will, further, assemble before the throne of God, a "great crowd that no man was able to number" as a New World Society, as spoken of in the Revelation.

WE HEREBY CLAIM the mantle passed from Russell to Rutherford to Knorr and proclaim ourselves to be:

The NEW WORLD SOCIETY 2024

A space where all true Christians can meet, free from the taint of religion, free from the hypocrisy evident in every church and Kingdom Hall, free from the soporific leadership of the entitled, free from both the traditions of Christendom and the culture of self-exaltation evident within the CCJW.

Logically, morally, the Governing Body must respond, as follows:

TO WHOM IT MAY CONCERN:

On the occasion of the publication of this book, we, the Governing Body of the Christian Congregation of Jehovah's Witnesses, say as follows:

• We apologize and accept responsibility for the errors that have been made over our tenure as stewards of Kingdom interests here on the earth

• We, as individual members of this Body, restate our commitment to the Kingdom Arrangement and pledge to fully support the new administration to whom we will pass the baton

• We, as a last act of faithful service, as a collective Body, will make the necessary arrangements for a hearing to be held at the Watchtower Branch facility in Georgetown Ontario in the very near future

- Said hearing will approximate, in importance and in substance, the hearing held in Jerusalem in the first century, when similarly important issues as those that face us now were discussed and resolved

- We will act to maintain good order within the true Christian congregation and its affiliated organization until such time as new leaders are appointed

- We will recuse ourselves from the process of debate and discussion which must take place to determine refinements, adjustments and the renewal that must take place within Jehovah's Arrangement here on earth

- We encourage all of you to act in good conscience as you follow the lead that Jehovah will provide from now until the end of this Old World Order

We thank Jehovah and His Son for the privilege we have shared, together with all of you, in doing our very best in service to Him; and as we contemplate our heavenly reward, we fondly say:

Praise Jehovah, the Almighty God and his Son, Jesus Christ, our Lord, our Saviour, Our King, all good-hearted peoples of the earth!

With deep respect and humility, we are,

Yours in faith,

APPENDIX:

ITEM

No. Pages

A - Exhibit, MW Affidavit - letter M. Warburton to Governing Body - 17-01-04   4

B - Exhibit, MW Affidavit - letter M. Warburton to R. Duncan - 97-08-11   1

C - Exhibit, MW Affidavit - letter R. Jung to S. Oostdyk - 16-02-15   1

D - Exhibit, MW Affidavit - letter P. Brumley to K. Morimoto - 16-09-20   2

E - Exhibit, MW Affidavit - letter M. Warburton to Governing Body - 19-09-14   3

F - Attach#1, MW to Lett letter - letter K. McVicar to NB elders - 23-02-08   4

G - Attach#2, MW to Lett letter - letter D. Gnam to K. McVicar - 23-02-22   2

H - Attach#3, MW to Lett letter - letter M. Warburton to D. Gnam - 23-02-23   2

A

121 - 762 Upper James St.
Hamilton ON
L9C 3A2

January 04, 2017

Governing Body
The Christian Congregation of
Jehovah's Witnesses
25 Columbia Heights
Brooklyn NY 11201 - 2483
UNITED STATES of AMERICA

by fax 718.560.5101

Dear brothers,

I hereby make request for full investigation of the following questions, according to law.

Theocratic Laws demands that you, the Governing Body, answer for the conduct of the Congregation and its' Elders within the CCJW, as well as for the conduct of the Circuit Overseers, Canada Branch personnel and the respective Legal Departments at Georgetown ON and Patterson NY who administer the Watchtower Bible & Tract Societies which operate under the respective laws of Canada and the United States.

It is my preference to appeal to you under Theocratic Law; I have corresponded with you and with all of the above named entities over a period of 19 years. I have specifically corresponded with your General Counsel, Philip Brumley, on 4 occasions, starting with my letter of September 08, 2016; I have copied Brumley on correspondence to you over the last 3 months. All of this has been in an effort to alert you and your legal representatives to the weight of evidence that I have accumulated as to mistreatment I and my family have endured within the CCJW.

Here are the questions which require your consideration and which require explanation:

In the period 1990 - 1992, why did David Dorman and Thomas Linfield, Elders of the Parkton Congregation, Moncton, NB, take the position that Robert and Douglas Duncan could engage in slanderous and defamatory talk against me to family members and to they themselves? Why would they refuse my repeated requests to sit in on a discussion between myself and my in-laws, as at Matt. 18 : 15-17?

In July 1997, why did Colin Cummings and Roy Corbett, Elders of the Scarlett Heights Congregation, Toronto, ON, refuse to assist in application of Matt. 18 : 15-17 when presented with my letter to Robert Duncan?

GovBod/17-01-04
Page 2

In the summer of 1997, when I went to the Service Desk in Georgetown with my brother-in-law Robert Duncan Jr., why did Rodney Jung, when advised of a consistent pattern of conduct in allowing slander to go unchecked, on the part of elders in both New Brunswick and Ontario, promise to take action but fail to do so?

In August of 1997, why did Grant Sonmor, Circuit Overseer, affirm the Scarlett Heights Body in allowing the slander to run its course, resulting in the decimation of my family?

In September 1997, why did Colin Cummings of the Scarlett Heights Body fail to mitigate the situation and fail to invoke brotherly discussion, as I had requested and as at Matt 18 :15-17, when given foreknowledge of an ambush contrived on the advice of a worldly lawyer, by Robert Duncan, Carol Duncan and Kathleen Warburton against me?

In their letter of January 25, 1999, why did the Service Desk at Georgetown, under signature of the Watchtower Bible & Tract Society of Canada, refer me back to the Body of Elders of the Royal York Congregation, claiming no knowledge of the continuing problem of slander?

On November 1, 1999, after a regular Sunday morning meeting, why did Elders of the Royal York Congregation, Peter Schweller and Jonathan Arnett, ask in a meeting in the KH library, ask me to confess to sexual molestation of a retarded boy at a social event the night prior, without benefit of my accuser being present?

Why, after interviewing the alleged victim, and after the charge having been withdrawn, did said false accuser continue to enjoy platform privileges in the congregation? Why, when they accommodated my request, as at Matt. 18:15-17, for a meeting with Carol Down, mothe rof the accuser, who actually delivered the accusation as fact, did Peter Schweller subvert the meeting by assigning an agenda to the discussion? What scriptural precedent or principle directs that an Elder conducts and limits such a meeting, especially in view of the longstanding problem between myself and the Duncans, as known to Schweller?

In the summer of 2001, why did Donald Gordon and Daniel Digaetano, Elders of the Broadway Congregation in Welland, ON, meet secretly with my wife, Sherri Moir, without my knowledge or permission? Why, in harmony with Matt. 18:15-17, did these elders not respect theocratic procedure in this regard?

In the fall of 2001, why did Elders of the Cooks Mills, Welland, ON congregation provide assistance to and support Sherri Moir in Family Court in Welland?

On January 1, 2007, after numerous hearings in regard to my reinstatement, why was I asked to pen a letter to the Aldershot Body of Elders by Robert Hicks, chairman of a committee of the

GovBod/17-01-04
Page 3

Victoria Gardens Body, other than as a signal of acknowledgment of repentance for my own sins?

Why, according to Ernest Downes, Chairman of the Aldershot committee, did the Service desk in Georgetown, ON specifically prohibit acceptance of my plea?

In May 2010, why did the Service Desk in Georgetown subvert my attempts in Family Court in Fredericton, NB, to affirm my right as a father to educate my daughter in the knowledge of Jehovah God? Why did the Service Desk dispatch Jayden MacEwan to prevent local Elsers from testifying to counteract slander against Jehovah God and the Shediac Congregation, which slander was delivered under oath by Sherri Moir, in order to prevent our daughter from attending the Kingdom Hall or even entering into discussion about "the Truth"?

Why was my letter of August 19, 2012, addressed to Michaewl Goodwin, Circuit Overseer, in which I asked that the policy regarding reinstatement be respected, ignored? Why did Goodwin not direct that a new committee, in my new congregation, hear my plea for reinstatement?

Why, when I approached Goodwin at a Circuit Assembly the following month, was he adamant that only a committee of the Victoria Gardens congregation could consider my plea?

Why, in the summer of 2013, were my aged parents removed from the vicinity of my care, without consultation, by the Circuit Overseer David Cohen and my sister, Miriam Cohen? Why did the Service Desk in Georgetown direct the Body of Elders in Summerside, PEI, to cooperate with and enable this abduction, in violation of Family Law?

Why, after a year of faithful meeting attendance at the Aldershot Congregation over the year 2016, after demonstration that I am living in harmony with Jehovah's standards, has my plea for reinstatement been spurned?

Why would Daniel Trigianni, Elder of the Aldershot Congregation, insist that, in order for reinstatement to be considered, I must forgive all those who injured my loved ones, as above, without benefit of the exercise of Matt. 18:15-17 towards them?

Why would Brian Vlaanderem, Elder of the Aldershot Congregation, imply that, in order for reinstatement to be considered, I must stop all efforts to bring these matters to light?

Why would Brian Vlaanderen insist that I should focus only on the spiritual needs of my daughter, when such is practically impossible, given the interference of the Broadway Elders, the Cook's Mills Elders and the Service desk in Georgetown?

GovBod/17-01-04
Page 4

Brothers, these are not passing or isolated matters of concern - there is a pattern of conduct at work! The costs incurred have been immense. I ask that you consider these matters with a view to answering the why's as presented, both with a view to redressing my own situation and as to considering any enhancements to policy and practice that might prevent such occurrence to others.

Thank you for your consideration

With brotherly love,

Mark Warburton
Cc. P. Brumley

B

FROM:	MARK WARBURTON	TO:	BOB DUNCAN, SR.
	40 Bexley Cres.		
	City of York, Ontario		
	M6N 2P7		

DATE: August 11, 1997   FAX#:   416 259-5804

NO. PAGES: 1 only

RE: OUR PROBLEM

Dear Bob,

I sincerely regret your refusal to meet with me at 4:00 p.m. last Thursday to follow-up on our discussion of the same morning. It is best to resolve disputes as soon as possible after they arise; However, there might be some value in having let the matter rest for a period of time so that we could all consider the points raised. Hopefully, this will contribute to a successful repair of our relationship, both familial and brotherly.

Believe me when I tell you, as I did Thursday morning, that I want to enlist your assistance in trying to arrest and turn around the damage being done to your daughter, my wife. I willingly acknowledge my contribution to this situation; My contribution, however, is now in the past chronologically, if not in mind.

As for your accusation, that I am a liar, I would ask that you specify to me the lies that I have told. It seems, from your reference to Martha Simmons, that you are under the impression that I lied about, or misrepresented, this matter. I only have one recollection of a conversation (with your wife) in your presence, at which the matter of my distress over the situation arising from my involvement with Martha was discussed. In fact, it was at that time that I first tried to enlist your help, as I do now. My recollection is that at that time, too, you were disinclined to get involved. Hence, my question........what lie have I told you? Or even others?

In view of the slanderous nature of this remark, and in view of your refusal to resolve this matter person-to-person, I am asking that you agree to a meeting with one or two impartial witnesses present. I believe that Olavi would still be willing to agree to sit in with us for this purpose, if you are agreeable. If you would like to nominate some other person, I would gladly consider it.

As for the suggestion that this should be treated as a family matter, I do not see it as such, especially in view of your remark that you no longer consider me to be family.

I will wait 24 hours to hear from you.

With great concern and agape,

C

Christian Congregation of Jehovah's Witnesses
Congrégation chrétienne des Témoins de Jéhovah

PO Box/C. P. 4100, Georgetown, Ontario L7G 4Y4, Canada
Telephone/Téléphone: 905-873-4100 Fax/Télécopieur: 905-873-4554

February 15, 2016

Mr. Sean Oostdyk
Van der Woerd, Faber & Oostdyk
1025 Waterdown Road
Burlington, ON L7T 1N4

Re: Mark Warburton – Reinstatement Process

Dear Mr. Oostdyk :

We received your letter dated February 5, 2016, concerning your client's request for information regarding the process to be reinstated as one of Jehovah's Witnesses.

Contrary to your assertions, Jehovah's Witnesses' reinstatement process is consistent and transparent; it is outlined in the book "Organized to Do Jehovah's Will" under the section "Reinstatement". All Jehovah's Witnesses receive this book before they are baptized. Moreover, Mr. Warburton, as a former congregation elder, is familiar with the reinstatement process, and the necessary "fruits that befit repentance" he must demonstrate to qualify.—Luke 3:8; 2 Corinthians 7:10, 11.

Please refer Mr. Warburton to the book "Organized to Do Jehovah's Will" in his possession, it contains all the information he requires.

Yours truly,

Rodney Jung
Superintendent of Ministers and Evangelists

D

WATCH TOWER
Bible and Tract Society of Pennsylvania
Legal Department
100 Watchtower Drive, Patterson, NY 12563-9204, U.S.A.
Phone: (845) 306-1000 Fax: (845) 306-0709

September 20, 2016

Karen Morimoto
Startek, Peglar & Calcagni
Barristers and Solicitors
952 Queenston Road
Stoney Creek, ON L8G 1B7

Re: Your client—Mr. Mark Warburton

Dear Ms. Morimoto:

We are in receipt of your letter dated September 9, 2016, addressed to the Governing Body c/o Legal Department at Patterson, NY. We are also in receipt of Mr. Warburton's personal letters dated May 12 and September 17, 2016, addressed to the Governing Body.

You state that the local "elders are not willing, or able, to resolve" Mr. Warburton's "issues." You also believe that the local elders need "guidance and leadership." Please advise Mr. Warburton that the Governing Body does not become involved in determining whether someone may continue to be associated with Jehovah's Witnesses. These matters are cared for by local elders and, as necessary, regional offices such as the Georgetown office.

As you may know, numerous elders have tried to address the issues raised by Mr. Warburton. If Mr. Warburton truly wants to become re-associated with Jehovah's Witnesses, we believe he knows what he must do. But if not, the local body of elders in the Aldershot Congregation, where he has been attending some meetings, are in the best position to explain this to him. These spiritually qualified elders are familiar with Mr. Warburton and are very well versed in the scriptures and the beliefs and practices of Jehovah's Witnesses. On the other hand, if Mr. Warburton simply wants to expose what he perceives as "troubling conditions in the congregations" then there is little that any congregation elders can do to help him.

Since this is a spiritual matter, we believe that it is in Mr. Warburton's best interests to handle this matter spiritually, rather than legally. In this regard, in *Lakeside Colony of Hutterian Brethren v Hofer* [1992] 3 S.C.R. 165 at paras 6, 64, Justice Gonthier wrote that the courts are "slow to exercise jurisdiction over the question of membership in a voluntary association, especially a religious one," holding they only do so "where a property or civil right turns on the question of membership." The Court explained that "the difficulty of understanding tradition and custom [of the religious community] is really one reason to avoid assuming jurisdiction in the first place."

Karen Morimoto
Re: Your client—Mark Warburton
September 20, 2016
Page 2

The guarantee of freedom of religion found in s. 2(a) of the *Charter* protects both individuals and religious communities and institutions. In *Loyola High School v Quebec (Attorney General)*, 2015 SCC 12 at paras 43, 44, the Supreme Court of Canada emphasized the state duty of neutrality: "A secular state does not—and cannot—interfere with the beliefs or practices of a religious group unless they conflict with or harm overriding public interests." The majority in *Loyola High School* warned, "measures which undermine the character of lawful religious institutions and disrupt the vitality of religious communities represent a profound interference with religious freedom." (*Supra* note 31 at para 67.)

Accordingly, we urge Mr. Warburton to pursue re-association and to speak with the local elders if he truly does not know what he has to do in this regard. While Mr. Warburton may do as he wishes, he should understand that neither the Governing Body, nor any representative of the Governing Body, will grant him an audience. As stated above, the Governing Body does not involve itself in these matters. Mr. Warburton will simply be asked to leave and if he does not comply, he shall be treated as a trespasser and the appropriate authorities will be contacted. We truly hope that such does not occur and that you can counsel your client to pursue this matter spiritually with the local elders in accordance with Jehovah's Witnesses' beliefs and practices for re-association.

Thank you for your efforts to assist Mr. Warburton and for taking the time to write to us.

Very truly yours,

Philip Brumley
General Counsel

PB:dsr

E

1127 Main St. - B138
Moncton NB E1C 1H1 CANADA

September 14, 2019

Governing Body
Christian Congregation of Jehovah's Witnesses
1 Kings Drive
Tuxedo Park NY 10987 USA

Dear sirs,

The article entitled "Is All Complaining Condemned?" (WT 12/01/97) contains the following notable quotes:

"Jesus made mention of an unrighteous judge who begrudgingly meted out justice to an oppressed widow......we too may have to persist in our complaints......"

"Situations will arise [within the Christian congregation] that give cause for a measure of complaint and that call for a remedy."

"Complaints should be made in the proper spirit and to the proper authority......it would be inappropriate to complain about some situation......inside...... the congregation to a person who had no authority or ability to help."

Please recognize that I have presented a legal case to the collective Elder Body of the CCJW, as at Psalm 43:1 - "do conduct my legal case against a nation not loyal"; and my continuing efforts constitute an appeal for attention to this matter by your Body. It is now clear that your Body, and only the Governing Body, has the authority to deal with this matter.

Local Elder Bodies in the congregations are comprised of men who follow the maxim that the Faithful & Discreet Slave, of Matt 24:45, provides direction in all matters; that anyone who complains is missing this bigger picture; that the antidote for injustice in the congregation is cultivation of a positive attitude; and that, far from elders acting to rectify a matter, any such complainers must be quarantined.

Overseers of the work of Jehovah's Witnesses, Branch personnel and travelling Overseers, direct Elder Bodies in the application of policy and procedure; they perpetuate an unbending conformity to the rule of order, the traditions and the hierarchy that has been designated as "the Organization". When presented with a conscientious concern of an elder which runs counter to the democratically established position of any Body of Elders, such an elder will be heard and then asked to conform to the Body, under threat of loss of his privilege of eldership.

GovBody/19-09-15
Page 2

Lawyers who represent you, elders themselves, effectively use the law code of the Old World Order to blunt any request for answerability to any external authority; or, indeed, to subvert the questionings of any individual for whom the workings of the Organization have caused, or contributed to, injury. It is the greatest irony, and a strong comparable, that these same lawyers use the same law code of the Old World Order on your behalf, to call into question injustices perpetrated by worldly authorities against the Organization.

There is no place or facility within this structure to consider a solitary voice raised up in alarm.

It should be noted here that when those injured by the practices of others bring a party to any Court, secular or otherwise, the desired result is not simply for setting the record straight, nor even is it compensation for damage, but, rather, it is that hurtful practices are identified and corrected, for the ongoing benefit of all parties. Your unwillingness to submit to good faith examination of the Organization, either internally or externally, bespeaks an insular culture within the Organization that has seen the CCJW/WTB&TS regress from the welcoming and open movement that arose under the guidance and direction of Charles Taze Russell to the closed, inward looking, hierarchical, authoritarian and sometimes hurtful religion that it has become.

Here is the substance of my legal case:

With no attempt to shirk my own culpability, I have confessed to my own mistakes and my appropriate attitude, my repentance, has been acknowledged; and, yet, I have been denied application of the ransom sacrifice; on three occasions local elders have been directed by the Canada Branch to withhold reinstatement. Judgment has been rendered based on prejudicial religiosity, hearsay and slander; this is a tragedy in my life; and, notwithstanding my pleas to you, and to others, my matters have been covered up in the interest of religious solidarity.

Correspondence has been directed in timely fashion (for over 25 years; as problematic situations arose they were duly summarized in writing, with a view to remediation) to my own Body(ies) of Elders, to my Circuit Overseer(s), to Branch personnel, to WTB&TS lawyers and to the Governing Body. My straightforward requests, prior to my disfellowshipping in October 2002, were for help in application of the procedure outlined at Matthew 18:15-17. The principle which formed the basis of my requests was the principle of headship; my goal was to engage various parties in the congregation, including elders, who engaged in slander against me; my motive was to preserve my family; your negligence in these matters cost me both my family and my standing as a JW. Since October 2002, I have sought remedy by a forensic examination of these matters; my goal has been to highlight a pattern of injustice fostered by the practices of the Organization, even today; my motive has been the remediation of a closed system of worship that has been damaging, even death-dealing, to many adherents of the Christian faith.

GovBody/19-09-15
Page 3

In regard to the "proper spirit" referred to in the WT article from 12/97, my tone has variously been beseeching, scolding and complaining. I need you to understand that, at all times, in raising these matters I have demonstrated loyalty by directing my concerns to the proper authority. Now, when the trajectory of all of my cumulative messaging leads to a suggestion, at it's extreme, that the Faithful Slave has morphed into the Evil Slave referred to at Matthew 24:48, it can be, and has been, ascribed as a bad attitude on my part; on the other hand, it can also be received as a message of concern for your claimed standing as duly appointed representatives of the Great God, Jehovah, and, indeed, for your own personal standing before Him.

As for biblical precedent upon which I have drawn, the Greek Scriptures contain letters penned by individual elders, most extensively by Paul, setting out defects they identified as harmful to the community exercise of Christianity; no letter was penned by any collective Body; the singular reference to a Body formed to consider questions of Jewish influence within the congregation resulted in a decision prefaced by a stated desire NOT to impose extensive legalistic conditions on Christian worship. Jeremiah, amongst others, was tasked with delivering reproving messages to the leaders of God's people in Israel; men such as Amos were raised up from outside the leadership structure to draw attention to an errant course. Jeremiah was thrown down a well for his forthrightness. I write from a 12 year detention in a well of ostracism and pain, imposed by elders of the Christian congregation.

In seizing stewardship of the Christian movement; in elevating your own personal approach to worship; in crafting a controlling, religious structure; in your failure to respond to my concerns, and those of others, as brothers; in the contravention of your claimed privilege as a Faithful & Discreet Slave; you and your Overseers, Branch and Circuit, have missed opportunity to re-invigorate the movement started by CT Russell, by applying the soporific weight of your authority, rather than preserving the peer-to-peer, collective version of Christianity evident both in the first century and in the renewal initiated, by Divine Authority, by Charles Taze Russell.

Please consider, again, Micah 6:8 - "What is Jehovah requiring of you? ..... [but] to exercise justice...". I ask for judicial hearing, with you and against you, in the Court of the Grand Theocrat, Jesus Christ.

Regards

Mark Warburton
        cc. D. Gnam, How & Assoc./P. Brumley, WTB&TS Pennsylvania

F

*C.A. Haché Law
20 Marr Rd., Suite 200
Rothesay, NB E2E 2R5
katie@cahachelaw.ca
Phone: (506) 216-8800
Fax: (506) 717-0281

WITHOUT PREJUDICE

February 8ᵗʰ, 2023

Via Registered Mail

Mr. Shane Houle	Mr. James Horsman	Mr. David Liebel
204 NB-865	205 Blythwood Ave #12	2447 Candace St.
Norton, NB	Riverview, NB	Saint John, NB
E5T 1H2	E1B 2G7	E2J 2Z8

Dear Sirs:

Re: Attendance at meetings by Mr. Mark Warburton
         Our File No.: 23011

I have been retained by Mr. Mark Warburton to communicate with you in your respective capacities as respective spokespersons of the Sussex, Riverview and Bayside Congregations of Jehovah's Witnesses.

Mr. Warburton is seeking information regarding the decision to prohibit his attendance at meetings, and the refusal of your congregations to assemble committees to meet with him to discuss his continued disfellowship.

Background

On or about October 2002, Mr. Warburton was disfellowshipped by a judicial committee of the congregation of Aldershot, Burlington, Ontario.

Since being disfellowshipped, Mr. Warburton has applied for reinstatement on the following occasions and with the following results:

- **Fall 2005** – Application to the Victoria Gardens congregation;
    - On or about January 2007, the committee recommended a letter of plea to the Aldershot committee.
    - On or about February 2007, the committee informed Mr. Warburton that his plea was refused.
- **Summer 2008** – Application to the Shediac congregation;
    - Mr. Warburton was informed he could only apply for reinstatement to the Victoria Gardens congregation.
- **2010** – Application to Salisbury congregation.
    - Mr. Warburton was informed he was not welcome to apply for reinstatement there.
- **2016** – Application to the Aldershot committee;

           *Practicing as Charles A. Haché Professional Corporation

*C.A. Haché Law
20 Marr Rd., Suite 200
Rothesay, NB E2E 2R5
katie@cahachelaw.ca
Phone: (506) 216-8800
Fax: (506) 717-0281

- o After attending meetings, including meeting with the Aldershot committee 4 or 5 times, over the course of 9 months, Mr. Warburton's plea for reinstatement was refused.
- **2018/2019** – Application to Riverview congregation;
  - o Mr. Warburton was informed that the "implied invitation" to attend meetings was revoked on or about Fall 2019.
- **2020** – Application to Amherst congregation;
  - o Mr. Warburton's request for a hearing to lead to reinstatement was denied.
- **October 2022** – Application to Bayside congregation;
  - o Mr. Warburton attended meetings in person and remotely from August 2022 to October 2022.
  - o After making an application for reinstatement in writing, Mr. Warburton was informed by Mr. Lebel via telephone that the "implied invitation" to attend meetings was withdrawn.
- **December 2022** – Attendance at Sussex congregation;
  - o Mr. Warburton attended 5 meetings at the Kingdom Hall in Sussex from December 17th, to January 2023.
  - o On or about January 3rd, 2023, Mr. Warburton was informed by Mr. Houle via telephone that the "implied invitation" to attend meetings was withdrawn.

Over the course of these many applications for reinstatement, Mr. Warburton has never been provided with reasons for the rejection of his plea.

Reinstatement

It is Mr. Warburton's understanding that for a disfellowshipped member to be reinstated, he must demonstrate repentance, which includes regular attendance at meetings.

Prior to and throughout the process of each of Mr. Warburton's applications for reinstatement, Mr. Warburton has sought to attend meetings of Jehovah's Witnesses. Prior to 2019, rejections of Mr. Warburton's applications for reinstatement were not accompanied by prohibitions by the Elders to continue to attend meetings.

Mr. Warburton has been attempting to follow the requirements as set by the Watch Tower Bible and Tract Society of Canada, the Christian Congregation of Jehovah's Witnesses, and your congregations and yet, has been refused at every turn. Each time he is led to believe he has begun to make progress, a different congregation closes the door in his face with no explanation of his falter.

When reviewing the perspective regarding disfellowshipped individuals, the website, JW.org sets out:

Disfellowshipped individuals may attend our religious services. If they wish, they may also receive spiritual counsel from congregation elders. The goal is to help each individual once more to qualify to be one of Jehovah's Witnesses. Disfellowshipped people who reject

*C.A. Haché Law
20 Marr Rd., Suite 200
Rothesay, NB E2E 2R5
katie@cahachelaw.ca
Phone: (506) 216-8800
Fax: (506) 717-0281

improper conduct and demonstrate a sincere desire to live by the Bible's standards are always welcome to become Jehovah's Witnesses again.

https://www.jw.org/en/jehovahs-witnesses/faq/shunning/

It is Mr. Warburton's position that a prohibition from attending meetings is against the prescribed goals of the Jehovah's Witnesses. Mr. Warburton submits he has been seeking counsel from the elders of your individual congregations in the hope of qualifying to be a Jehovah's Witness once more.

Defamation

The time period that Mr. Warburton has been allowed to attend meetings has decreased dramatically in the last year between your congregations. Mr. Warburton had only attended 5 meetings before receiving a call from Mr. Houle indicating his implied invitation to attend meetings was revoked. Mr. Warburton had not even made an application for re-instatement with the Sussex congregation before receiving the call on January 3rd, 2023. Mr. Warburton had not even provided his phone number to Mr. Houle, he had provided it only to Mr. Lawson Porter, an Elder at the Sussex congregation.

Mr. Warburton submits that there has been communication between either yourselves or other Elders within your congregation, discrediting himself, which has led to his most recent prohibition from attending meetings.

Mr. Warburton has not been privy to these communications, but based on his prohibition from meetings, and, to his knowledge, the fact that he has not committed any offences against any member of your three congregations, Mr. Warburton alleges that these communications have been to degrade his reputation, and resulted in his continued shunning from the Jehovah's Witness community.

Having been a Jehovah's Witness from birth, the defamation perpetuated by yourselves has impacted not only Mr. Warburton's friendships within the church community but also has interfered and impeded his relationships with his family within the Jehovah's Witness community.

Mr. Warburton submits that these communications made by yourselves to each other or other third parties, and your persistent refusal to meet or contemplate his reinstatement as a Jehovah's Witness are evidence of a degradation of his character to those within the Jehovah's Witness community and is evidence that you have defamed Mr. Warburton.

Inquiries

Respectfully, rather than seek remedy in the Court system regarding the defamation issue, Mr. Warburton is seeking answers to the following questions regarding the recent prohibitions from attending meetings at your respective congregations:

1. Why were the prohibitions issued?

*Practicing as Charles A. Haché Professional Corporation

*C.A. Haché Law
20 Marr Rd., Suite 200
Rothesay, NB E2E 2R5
katie@cahachelaw.ca
Phone: (506) 216-8800
Fax: (506) 717-0281

2. Has Mr. Warburton been in contravention of any rules of conduct pertaining to your meetings or committed any offences that demonstrate he is in any way non-repentant?

3. What steps must Mr. Warburton take for his application for reinstatement to be heard by a committee within one of your congregations?

4. If you will not lift the prohibition to attend meetings, how can Mr. Warburton demonstrate repentance, and his dedication to being readmitted as a Jehovah's Witness?

I thank you for your attention to this matter.

Yours very truly,

C. A. HACHÉ LAW*

PER: Katie McVicar,
Associate

KMM/kmm

*Practicing as Charles A. Haché Professional Corporation

161

G

W. Glen How
& ASSOCIATES LLP

PO Box 40
13893 Highway 7 (courier)
Georgetown ON L7G 4T1
☎ 905-873-4545
📠 905-873-4522

David M. Gnam, CPA, CGA, LL.B.
dgnam@wghow.ca

February 22, 2023

Via Email

Katie McVicar
C.A. Haché Law
20 Marr Rd, Suite 200
Rothesay NB E2E 2R5
katie@cahachelaw.ca

Dear Ms. McVicar:

Re: Mark Warburton
        Your File No.: 23011

I am retained by Shane Houle, James Horsman, and David Liebel to reply to your letter dated February 8, 2023, regarding Mr. Mark Warburton's legal threats.

None of these three gentlemen are spokespersons for the Sussex, Riverview, and Bayside Congregations of Jehovah's Witnesses. They are three part-time volunteer ministers who are Mr. Warburton's current targets in his over 20 year campaign against the religious beliefs and practices of Jehovah's Witnesses.

Mr. Warburton previously engaged lawyers in Ontario (Ms. Karen Morimoto in 2015 and Mr. Sean Oostdyk in 2016) to make similar legal threats regarding his religious status and perceived defamation. The legal answer to these threats has not changed. The unanimous Supreme Court of Canada in *Highwood Congregation of Jehovah's Witnesses (Judicial Committee) v Wall*, 2018 SCC 26 at paragraph 12, held, Courts do not have the jurisdiction to review the decisions of religious groups or other voluntary associations if no legal rights (such as a property or contractual right) are at stake, and further: "Issues of theology are not justiciable." At paragraph 31, the Court went on to indicate the "negative impact" the Congregation's decision to disfellowship had on Mr. Wall's personal life "does not give rise to an actionable claim."

Mr. Warburton has always been informed why he was disfellowshipped, why he was not reinstated, and why he is no longer welcome to attend congregation meetings. He chooses to not hear what he does not agree with. Mr. Warburton's stalking and harassment of Lawson Porter, an elderly Jehovah's Witness in his 90's, reported to RCMP Constable Lemay last week, is ample reason for his not being welcome to attend meetings.

On Tuesday, February 21, 2023, the national coordinator of Jehovah's Witnesses in Canada patiently listened to Mr. Warburton and explained to him what he needed to do to be reinstated, beyond merely attending congregation meetings. In complete disrespect for what he had just been told, Mr. Warburton called back the same day with further calumnious allegations about Jehovah's Witnesses. Our clients and the national office of Jehovah's Witnesses in Canada will not respond further to Mr. Warburton's telephone calls or dunning letters. If Mr. Warburton pursues litigation, this letter will be brought to the attention of the court in support of a request for costs under Rule 59.02 of the New Brunswick *Rules of Court*.

Yours truly,

W. GLEN HOW & ASSOCIATES LLP

David M. Gnam

DMG/vb

H

569 Martha Avenue
Saint John NB
E2J 4L7

February 23, 2023

Mr. David Gnam
W. Glen How & Associates
P.O. Box 40
13893 Highway 7
Georgetown ON
L7G 4T1

Dear sir,

I am in receipt of your letter to my lawyer, Ms. Katie McVicar.

Your letter is factually incorrect, as follows:

1. All three gentlemen that you refer to placed calls to me and claimed to speak for their respective Bodies of Elders
2. All three gentlemen introduced the presence of a second elder on the line; there are witnesses available in this matter
3. I have no argument, whatsoever, with the beliefs of Jehovah's Witnesses
4. I have never issued any threat through any lawyer; I have asked for answers; my lawyers, Mr. Oostdyk, Ms, Morimoto, Ms. McVicar have been respectful and solicitous of answers to the conundrum which I face
5. My status has nothing to do with theology; it has to do with abuse of privilege and power
6. Defamation is the issue here, and my case is as different as chalk from cheese to that of Mr. Wall; Wall's claim was based on loss of fiduciary opportunity/my case is based on actual costs incurred; Mr. Wall's claim was based on loss of business/my case revolves around a callous alienation of affection

I advise you, sir, to not use inflammatory wording, such as "stalking" and "harassment"; such terms convey an effeminate predisposition towards authoritarian measures. Lawson Porter is my friend of 30 years.

In regard to my disfellowshipping, I was not informed of anything, I confessed; in regard to my many meetings in support of my request for reinstatement, you were not present. How dare you suggest that I was given reasons for the rejection of my plea?

JWgnam/23-02-23
Page 2

And may I point out, sir, that I was prohibited from attending meetings in Sussex long before Constable Lemay was, sadly, used by Mr. Porter. Certainly, my visit to Mr. Porter was not received well by him, AND IT WAS NOT THE REASON THAT MY ATTENDANCE AT MEETINGS WAS WITHDRAWN. Mr. Porter can speak for himself, can he not?....and if Lawson, himself, expressed concern, I would listen; I love that man.

Finally, sir, Mr. Warren Shewfelt does not have the courage to put me in my place. He is a milquetoast, sir, he did not say one word of rebuttal, to my claims.

You, sir, have not heard the last of this matter; your arrogant threats, thrown from your position of presumed advantage, will come back to haunt you.

Best regards,

Mark Warburton
Cc.   J. MacEwan
       K. McVicar

NEW WORLD SOCIETY 2024
48 Sackville St.
Shediac NB
E4P 2R2
CANADA
newworldsociety2024.net
FB - AdvocacyForANewWorldSociety
newworldsociety2024@gmail.com

The new, NEW WORLD SOCIETY!

www.newworldsociety2024.net

Made in the USA
Columbia, SC
29 July 2024

39149198R10093